A First
Course in
Mapwork

A First Course in Mapwork

Ralph T. Hare

Head of Geography, Dartington Hall School

To Brian,

Best Wishes

Ralph.

Macmillan Education
in association with the
Ordnance Survey

First published 1985
Published by
MACMILLAN EDUCATION LIMITED
Houndmills Basingstoke Hampshire RG21 2XS
and London
Associated companies throughout the world

Printed in Great Britain by
Redwood Burn Limited, Trowbridge, Wiltshire

British Library Cataloguing in Publication Data

Hare, Ralph
    A first course in mapwork.
    1. Maps   2. Great Britain — Maps
    I. Title
    912'.01'4   GA791

ISBN 0-333-32825-6

Contents

Ordnance Survey map extracts

The maps in this publication are reproduced from Ordnance Survey maps, with the permission of the Controller of Her Majesty's Stationary Office, Crown copyright reserved.

Teacher's Introduction

The aims of this book are to:

1 Provide a complete course in basic map reading for lower secondary school students
2 Develop the ability in students to conjure up an image of the landscape represented on a map
3 Help students to enjoy reading and using maps

The layout of the book

The book is divided into two main parts. Chapters 1 to 4 are chiefly, though not exclusively, devoted to teaching map reading concepts and skills. These chapters can be used together as a short introductory course, or be further subdivided for accommodation in existing courses. In chapters 5 to 10, the emphasis is on using these concepts and skills with map interpretation, because in this part students use maps to solve problems. Chapters 5 to 10 encourage students to visualise landscapes from maps. Each chapter is based on a geographical landscape theme that might be found in lower secondary school geography courses. This will ease integration of mapwork practice into the geography curriculum. Thus, the last six chapters follow no special sequence. In both parts of the book, the chapters are subdivided into units, which can form the basis of either single lessons or groups of lessons. Each unit contains many activities so it is hoped that teachers will select activities to suit their situation and to blend their own teaching methods with whatever is useful from this book. The text, as distinct from the activities, is an introduction to each group of activities and the unnumbered questions it contains are included in order to provoke student thought and discussion. Many of the activities lend themselves to group work and the overall accent is on activity rather than on exposition. Each chapter starts by telling students what they might expect to learn. Teachers can review these key sentences with students at the end of each chapter.

Chapter 1: As well as introducing the general concept of a map and specific map concepts (i.e. location, direction, scale, distance, height, symbol, and time and maps), this chapter also tries to develop the student's concept of space. Pupils often have diverse educational backgrounds, so this chapter of relatively simple activities can either be used to bring all students to a similar level of map understanding, or may be used as an introduction for lower ability pupils. If teachers wish to spend less time on model construction, then students can work in small groups to build the model between them, or the teacher could prepare a set of models to be stored and reused. Figures 1.5 and 1.6 are freed from copyright.

Chapter 2: In four units, this chapter explores four major map concepts and skills: symbol; distance; direction; and time in association with maps. Each unit can be seen as an extension to the introductory Chapter 1 or as a separate development of the ideas. In each unit, students are introduced to the main concept and their understanding is then deepened. Associated skills are explained and several opportunities for practice of these skills in different contexts are then offered. The unit on symbols acquaints students with the idea of symbols and the skill of decoding them as well as indicating their selective nature. In the unit on distance, the students meet the ideas of relative and absolute distance and then learn how to measure straight and crooked distances on maps. In a similar way the unit on direction introduces students to relative and absolute directions, moving from the egocentric viewpoint through the use of landmarks to the main compass points. Natural signposts are considered: for example, the fact that on the north side of trees in Britain, tree growth rings are larger and lichens are more likely to grow. The last unit develops the important idea that maps must be considered in the context of time.

Chapter 3: This comprises four units based on location, height, scale, and an activity that integrates the seven ideas and skills introduced in the first three chapters. The approach to each major concept is the same as in Chapter 2. The unit on height examines relative height, absolute height, contour, slope, and aspect. The idea of scale, use of scale, and drawing to scale usefully dovetail with the maps in Chapters 1 to 3.

Chapter 4: This contains three units. The first considers the variety of map-like images and their uses. The second unit concentrates on reinforcing and extending the map concepts and skills introduced in previous chapters. Lastly, a car rally exercise integrates the map ideas and skills of the first part of the book. Appendix A provides further information for this unit and is freed from copyright, as is Figure 4.13.

Chapter 5: This chapter could be integrated, for example, with course units on industry or South Wales and it contains sufficient material for several lessons. Examination of the nature of industrial landscapes is followed by their identification, mapping, analysis, and explanation. These activities teach industrial concepts, information about the Swansea Bay region and map skills with the 1:50 000 map, as a prelude to students creating imaginary industrial landscapes through their own industrial siting decisions. Table 5.2 is freed from copyright.

Chapter 6: This helps students to consider the problems of planning the provision and use of leisure facilities, at two different scales. There is also an opportunity to teach the usefulness of maps as an aid to recreation. Figure 6.1 is freed from copyright.

Chapter 7: This chapter presents the students with a real-life problem extracted from those actually experienced by the transport planning department of the British Sugar Corporation. Efficient route planning is a useful lifeskill for all to learn. The results included in Appendix B allow the teacher flexibility in the presentation of the problem.

Chapter 8: The central problem of this chapter is for students to locate and rescue an injured hill-walker from Ben Nevis. This requires map skills relating to the use of contours, as well as distance and direction. In Activity 8:2 the injured hill walker is located at grid reference 158731. A fresh position can be chosen by the teacher. This would entail the formulation of a different set of clues. Activity 8:3 lends itself to group work by students too. Figure 8.2 is freed from copyright.

Chapter 9: The main purpose of the cityscape chapter is to introduce students to the problems of a small part of inner city Coventry. They are asked to take on the role of planners to devise solutions to these problems and then to assume the roles of residents to help evaluate solutions. This sequence roughly follows the planning process. Data is based on the real situation in the early 1970s, although names, characters and some of the facts have been altered to make the activity simpler for students. Figures 9.6 and 9.7 are freed from copyright.

Chapter 10: The main activity in this chapter asks students to run an upland sheep farm for a year. They have to use map reading and interpretation skills to decide where to put their sheep at different times of the year. This involves recognising the grazing quality of different sections of the farm and matching this to the type of job to be done. In activity 10:7(6), the consequences of student decisions can be judged using Appendix C. Figure 10.16 is freed from copyright.

The following map of Britain shows the chapter, scale and location of the Ordnance Survey maps used in this book.

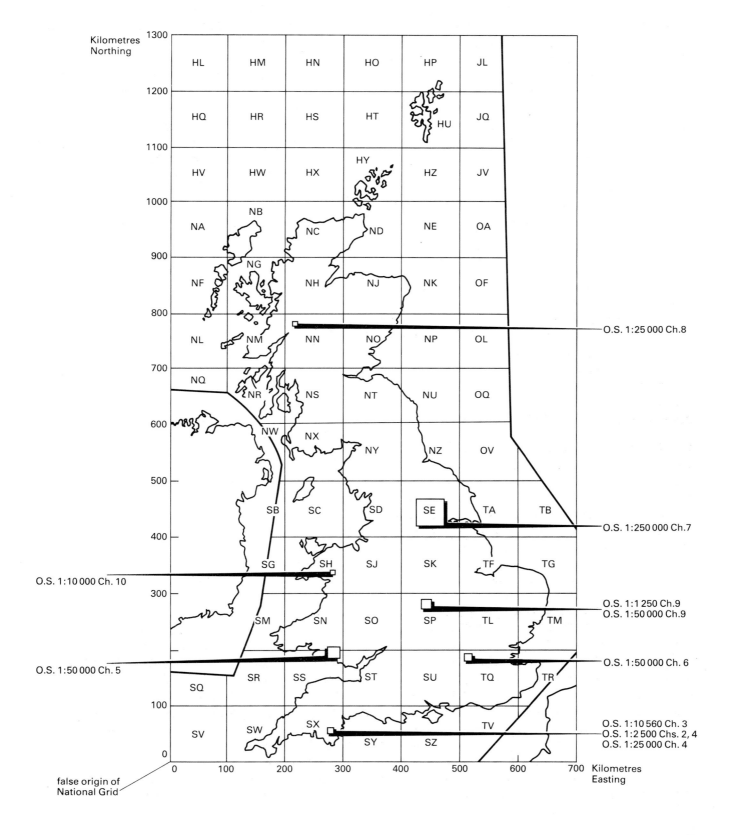

Kilometres Northing

O.S. 1:25 000 Ch.8

O.S. 1:250 000 Ch.7

O.S. 1:10 000 Ch. 10

O.S. 1:1 250 Ch.9
O.S. 1:50 000 Ch.9

O.S. 1:50 000 Ch. 5

O.S. 1:50 000 Ch. 6

O.S. 1:10 560 Ch. 3
O.S. 1:2 500 Chs. 2, 4
O.S. 1:25 000 Ch. 4

false origin of National Grid

Kilometres Easting

CHAPTER 1

Holiday in South Devon

What can you learn from this chapter?

It can:

1 Introduce you to part of the South Devon landscape
2 Help you understand the idea of geographical space
3 Clarify the idea of a map
4 Let you deal with several important ideas to do with maps

History, culture, beautiful scenery –
just some of the attractions of

Totnes and District

All you could wish for in a holiday – Totnes, famous since the 16th century and still a timber port nestling peacefully on the banks of the beautiful River Dart. The town has fine Elizabethan buildings, a Norman castle and a good selection of fascinating shops.

Nearby Dartington Hall is a centre for the arts, with concerts during the summer and superb gardens open to the public all the year round.

Totnes lies halfway between a choice of glorious beaches and the rugged wilderness of southern Dartmoor. It also has an indoor swimming pool, tennis and a choice of restaurants. The nightlife of Torbay is only 20 minutes drive away.

Easy access from London and the Midlands by motorway to Exeter and express dual carriageway A38 to within 4 miles of Totnes.

The area is filled with picturesque towns and villages – just waiting to be explored!

▲ Figure 1.1 An advertisement for Totnes and District

A model holiday

Daydream for a moment. Imagine the school summer term has finished and that you and your family have chosen to visit South Devon for a holiday. Use a wall map or atlas to find the position of the small, historic town of Totnes, South Devon. The advertisement in Figure 1.1 is designed to make the area sound appealing. Which aspects of the holiday would attract different members of your family?

Daydream further. Suppose that your family spots a second advertisement, Figure 1.2, and you choose to stay in this cottage for your holiday. What makes this house and its surroundings sound so attractive?

Dartington
Sleeps 5 to 7

Lounge, dining room, kitchen, 3 bedrooms, bathroom, television, piano, patio, colourful garden, garage, shed

14th century thatched cottage in the pretty hamlet of Lownard. Ten minutes walk from Dartington village, which has a shop/post office and old thatched Public House with restaurant. Nearby Dartington Hall provides restaurant, craft

shops and beautiful gardens open to the public.
Nearest town: Totnes
Riding stables nearby.
No pets.

▲ Figure 1.2 A cottage for holiday renting

▼ Figure 1.4   Lownard hamlet

Lownard
Cottages

4 3 2   1

When you arrive, you are met by the owners of Lownard Cottage, Nick and Lyn Evans, and their children: Gareth, who is fourteen years old, and Meriel, who is eleven. You can see them in the photograph, Figure 1.3. They have lived in the house for ten years, having moved there from South Wales. For the month of August they are going away on holiday themselves, but they have stayed to welcome you.

The cottage is one of a small group of buildings which is shown in Figure 1.4. Together, they are called Lownard Hamlet. The first activity will let you examine your holiday hamlet in more detail.

▲ Figure 1.3   The Evanses

Activity 1:1

(a) Make your own model of Lownard Hamlet by cutting out the shapes of some of the buildings from a copy of Figure 1.5. Follow the instructions carefully.

(b) When you have made the models, look at the photograph of Lownard, Figure 1.4, and see where the buildings are positioned. Place your models in their correct positions to make a model of the hamlet on your desk.

(c) In what ways does your model differ from the PLAN of Lownard Hamlet, Figure 1.6? Think about:
(i) the place where you put each building;
(ii) the position of one building in relation to another;
(iii) the spacing between buildings;
(iv) the lines that the buildings follow.

(d) Finally, put your model buildings in the right places on a copy of the plan.

No doubt one of the first things you do on arrival is to explore the hamlet from one end to the other. The next activity will lead you on a route through Lownard in a particular direction.

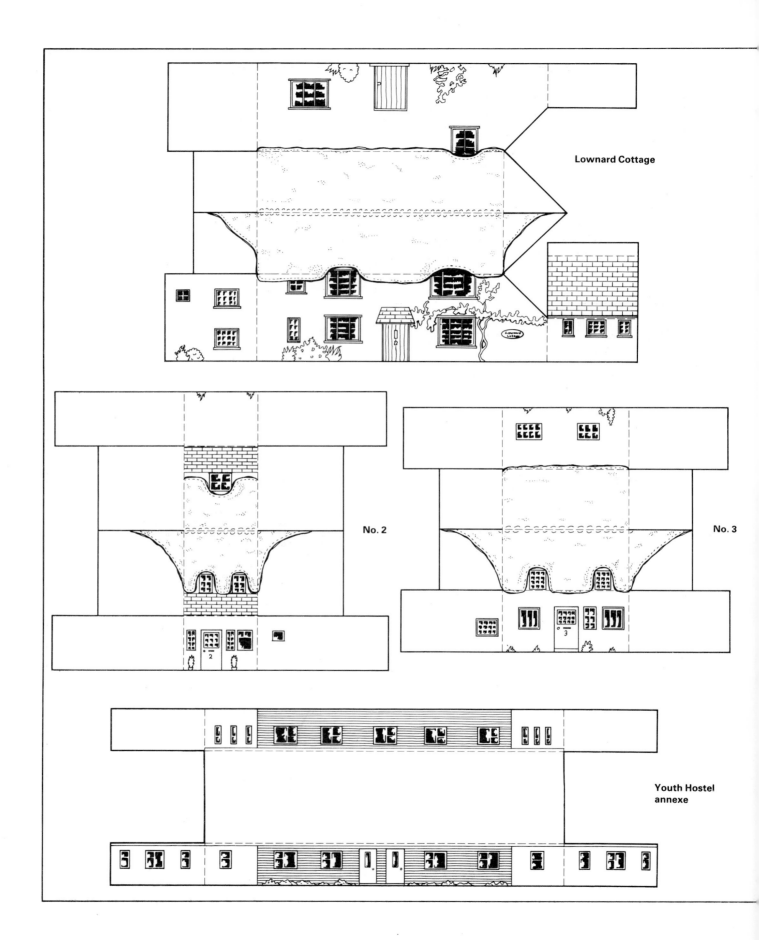

Lownard Cottage

No. 2

No. 3

Youth Hostel
annexe

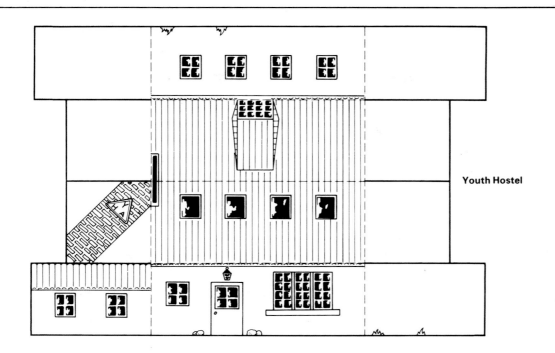

Youth Hostel

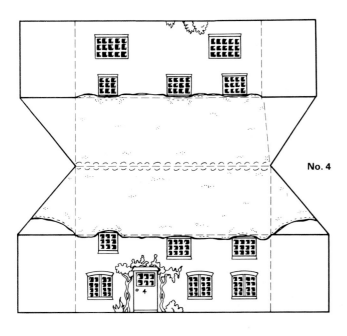

No. 4

How to make the models

Use a copy of this figure to make the model buildings. You could colour them first if you like.

Cut out the buildings along the thick lines, and fold them along the dotted lines. Fold first along the middle of the roof, and stick part A over part B. Then fold in the end walls and stick part C over part D.

Fold the roof of the extension to Lownard Cottage and tuck it under the gable end.

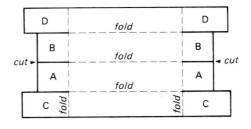

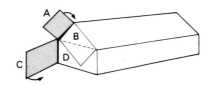

Figure 1.5   Cut-outs for the model of Lownard hamlet

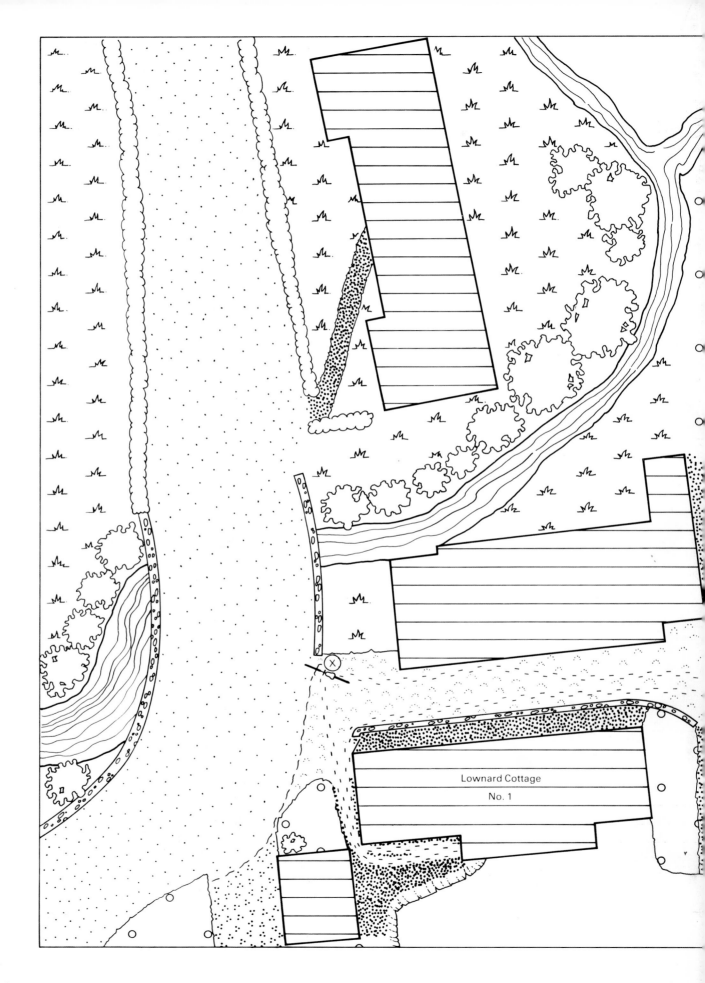

Lownard Cottage

No. 1

KEY

greenhouses

veg. plot

veg. plot

Y

fence

new garden sheds and garages

No. 2

No. 3

No. 4

N

Figure 1.6   A plan of Lownard hamlet

9

▲ Figure 1.7

▲ Figure 1.8

▲ Figure 1.9

▲ Figure 1.10

▲ Figure 1.11

Activity 1:2

(a) The five photographs, Figures 1.7 to 1.11, show the sequence of views you would see on a walk through Lownard Hamlet. Study Figure 1.7 and decide where your walk begins. Then trace the route on the plan with your finger, using the photographs as references.

(b) Decide exactly where each photograph was taken and neatly label each point on your copy of the plan.

(c) Study each photograph and, using the buildings as guides, decide in which direction each photograph was taken. Draw short arrows from the points labelled in Activity 1:2(b) to show these directions on your plan.

(d) Describe this walk in words, referring especially to your surroundings and to changes of direction.

(e) Describe a walk within your school.
(i) Choose one point at each end of your school and describe the route you would take to get from one point to the other.
(ii) Say why you chose this route.
(iii) Think of other ways (apart from written or spoken words, or photograph sequences) to describe a route to someone.

Activity 1:3

(a) You decide to phone a friend to tell them about your first impressions on arriving at Lownard. Choose a partner and imagine that they are on the other end of a telephone line. Tell them about Lownard Cottage and where it is situated in the hamlet.

(b) You send a postcard to a different friend. This time, write down your description and location of the cottage. Remember that you do not have much space to write on a postcard. Keep your sentences short, but full of information.

A moment in time

A LANDSCAPE is the overall picture that you get when you look at any area of land. The area might be of any size and it includes all the natural and man-made features that you see. Figures 1.7 to 1.11 show landscapes in Lownard and by studying them you can find clues about their past use. Given these clues, who would you talk to and where would you go if you wanted to discover how Lownard looked a few hundred years ago?

Nick and Lyn think that their house is nearly 600 years old. They discovered a clue to its former use in a local library. There they found Figure 1.12, a page in an auctioneer's booklet. Lot 20 was sold for £150 in 1920 and the larger farm buildings were converted for people to live in.

Activity 1:4

(a) Compare the description of Lownard Cottage in Figure 1.2 with its description as a farmhouse in Figure 1.12. What changes have taken place? How has the inside altered? How do these changes show how people had different lifestyles at different times?

(b) Figure 1.2 is an advertisement to rent Lownard Cottage for a holiday. How would the advertisement differ if the house was being sold instead of rented? Design and illustrate your own advertisement, bearing in mind the sort of phrases that estate agents might use to sell the cottage.

LOT 20.

LOWNARD FARM
Situate about Two miles from Totnes, and comprising:—

Farmhouse
Containing Four Bedrooms, Two Sitting Rooms, Kitchen, Dairy, Scullery, Cellar, Pump House and Washhouse.

Farm Buildings
Consisting of Root House, Cow House, Four Pigs' Houses, Calves' House, Barn, Cow House, Stable for Three Horses and Loft, Cow House with Loft, Cart Linhay and Trap House.

Together with the

Enclosures of Pasture and Arable Land
In all about

26a 2r 8p

SCHEDULE.

No. on Plan.	Description.	A.	R.	P.
	IN DARTINGTON PARISH.			
340	Pasture	2	2	16
342	Arable	2	0	5
343	Do.	2	3	36
344	Pasture	2	1	24
345	Arable	3	0	9
346	Plantation	0	3	13
347	Orchard	1	2	8
348	Arable	3	2	9
349	Plantation and Quarry	0	2	35
350	Farmhouse, Buildings, etc.	0	2	6
534	Pasture	2	1	12
740	Do.	3	3	35
	Total A.	26	2	8

This Lot is in hand, and possession will be given on the 25th March, 1920.

Commuted Tithe, 5s. 3d. per acre.   Land Tax, £2 9s.

The Growing Timber is to be paid for by Purchaser at £

▲ Figure 1.12   A page from an auction booklet of 1920

Nowadays, the cottages are homes for 11 people. However, the building opposite Lownard Cottage has over 600 visitors every year! Why do you think this is so? What can you see in Figure 1.7 that tells you the present use of the old cowhouse? Not much disturbs the sleepy life of Lownard, but 75-year-old Maggie White, who lives in Cottage Number Four, can tell you of one memorable occasion. She remembers the disastrous fire in the Youth Hostel on 3rd March 1955.

Activity 1:5

(a) Look again at photographs of that building, and the model. What evidence shows that the building might have been badly burnt?

(b) Which building in Lownard is the newest one? Give reasons for your choice.

(c) In Lownard, as in any group of old buildings, there are other items of interest to look for to discover the past and present life of the hamlet. The cobbled surface in Figure 1.8 has been rutted by cart wheels over the years. Lownard Cottage's ageing front wall needs support, as shown in Figure 1.7.

Try some detective work in your local area. Search for interesting features on houses, in walls, on the ground and all around you. Draw simple sketches of them and try to explain the feature's significance. A description of the clue and its location can be put before the class to test for local knowledge and to see if they, too, can work out its importance.

So, landscapes are changing constantly, but with certain objects and features that survive through time. Your model and plan will contain some of the objects and features of Lownard Hamlet that have survived till now, but who knows how it will change in the future? For example, Nick is building a greenhouse in his garden, which does not appear on your model or on the plan.

Activity 1:6

Activity 1:6 will help you to record 'a moment in time' in Lownard Hamlet, as well as helping you to understand geographical space.

(a) Working around the model in groups of three or four, imagine that each of you is standing on a different hillside around the hamlet. Sketch the particular view that you are facing.

(b) Exchange your group's sketches with those of another group and look at their sketches. See if you can identify the direction each person in that group was facing when they drew their landscape.

Activity 1:7

(a) You are going to look forward in time now. The hamlet is very close to a stream. If the stream were to flood and rise one metre above its banks, which building(s) might be flooded? Why would all the buildings not be flooded? Put the label 'low ground' on the plan where flooding might occur.

(b) Which of the buildings are one storey and which are two storeys in height?

(c) In exploring the area, where could you go to get above the hamlet and look down on it (look at Figure 1.4)? Mark the place on the plan where the high ground rises. Lightly draw a line which seems to separate high and low ground.

Bird's eye view

Susan Jenkins delivers newspapers to the houses at Lownard. You meet her on the first morning of your holiday. Lownard is not really very big, but Susan complains about all the walking she has to do around such hamlets. She leaves her bicycle at point X on Figure 1.6 and her actual paces are also shown.

Activity 1:8

(a) What is the distance that Susan walks on her newspaper round? Count up the number of paces drawn on the plan of the hamlet. (You may find it easier to record each section of the walk separately.)

(b) How big is your classroom? Count up the number of your own paces needed to walk along one side of the room and down the next side. Compare these distances with the number of paces that Susan took along the end and the front of Lownard Cottage. Which is larger, your classroom or the cottage?

(c) Roughly how far, in paces, do you think each of the following journeys would be?
(i) Nick's walk from his front door to his vegetable garden at Point Y.
(ii) A guest's walk from the Youth Hostel dormitory (the low wooden building) to the hostel's front door.
(iii) The extra distance that Susan would have to walk if the people in Number 4 started taking newspapers.

(d) Each of Susan's paces is half a metre long.
(i) Work out the total distance she has to walk, in metres, on her Lownard paper round.
(ii) How big, then, is Lownard Cottage?
(iii) How big is your classroom?

(e) Look at just one of Susan's paces on the plan (that is, the length between two footprints). It is very tiny. How many times do you think that one of these tiny paces would fit into a full-sized pace of a half metre? Do you think it might be 40, 50, 200, 500, or 1000 times? In fact, a real-life pace is 200 times as long as a pace on the plan. So your answer should have been that the tiny pace would have fitted into the real life half-metre 200 times. This is called the SCALE of an object. The tiny pace is said to be drawn at a scale of 1:200.

(f) Guessing or estimating distances can be tricky. Test yourself by guessing five different distances in paces, somewhere in your home or school area. Then measure them in your own paces, taking care not to shorten or lengthen your strides to make your answers right!
(i) Which distances were you the nearest in estimating the correct answer and which were you furthest from the correct answer?
(ii) What are the strengths and weaknesses of this technique for describing and measuring distance?

While using the model you have probably leaned over and looked straight down onto it more than once. In real life we do not get many opportunities to take a bird's eye view of the landscape. So the overhead viewpoint may be unfamiliar to you.

Activity 1:9

(a) Study Figure 1.13, which shows a bird's eye view of several everyday objects. They are not necessarily the same size in relation to each other. Decide what the objects are.

(b) Choose objects and try to sketch what they would look like from a bird's eye view.

(c) Look at some buildings near your school or home and draw what they might look like from above. Choose the same buildings as someone else so that you can compare your completed sketches with theirs.

▼ Figure 1.13   A bird's eye view of some everyday objects

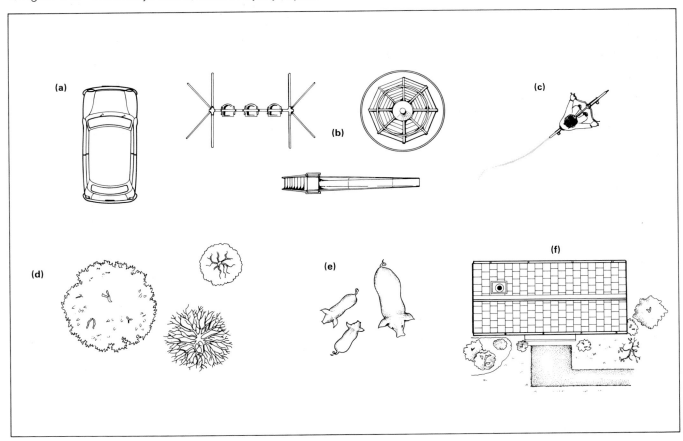

Activity 1:10

(a) Returning to the model of Lownard Hamlet, lean over and look at it directly from above. What things in the model have disappeared from your line of vision?

(b) What things can be seen much better?

If you take off the buildings, it leaves the flat piece of paper with outlines of the buildings on it. When it had the buildings on it, the model was three-dimensional. Now you have taken them off, the flat plan left is two-dimensional. This view of a small part of the world in miniature, from directly above, is also called a MAP. Plans usually show small pieces of the earth's surface while maps show larger areas.

Activity 1:11

(a) Using different colours for each group, shade the following things on your plan or map:
(i) all buildings and walls;
(ii) stream;
(iii) roads (tarmac, cobble and gravel);
(iv) paths;
(v) grass;
(vi) trees/hedgerows;
(vii) gardens (vegetables and flowers).

(b) In the space labelled KEY, shade the small boxes in the colours you have chosen and label them. Did you purposely choose colours to suit the features? If yes, say which ones. If no, suggest colours that might have been more appropriate.
(c) (i) You have used a three-dimensional model and a two-dimensional map to discover things about Lownard. Which did you enjoy using the most and why?
(ii) The map is handier for everyday use. What makes it so?
(iii) In what situations might the model be very useful? Explain why.

CHAPTER 2

Shinner's Bridge

What can you learn from this chapter?

It can:
1 Introduce you to the 1:2500 Ordnance Survey map
2 Help you to discover the meaning of symbols
3 Show you how to measure distances on a map
4 Indicate ways of finding directions
5 Suggest the importance of time and maps

Simple symbols

In the first chapter you learned about a small part of South Devon. Flying in a plane above that landscape you would see views like the one shown in Figure 2.1. On these black and white aerial photographs, certain items are easily recognised. For example, can you spot a car in a car park? Houses and fields are easy shapes to see, but what are the crops growing in the field in the background? Look at the larger buildings in the right centre of the picture. How are they used?

Activity 2:1

(a) Pick out examples of the following features in the photograph and note their positions, using the words:
　foreground; centre; background; left and right.
(i) A field of recently harvested wheat or barley (it looks almost white in the photograph).
(ii) A vegetable garden.
(iii) A clump of trees (they look dark grey and much like pieces of sponge rubber).
(iv) A field of grassland (which looks an even, grey colour).

(v) A white and grey, flat-topped office building.
(vi) Piles of timber in a saw mill.

Remember the patches of the map you coloured in Activity 1:11? The patches stood for buildings, gardens and so on. The different colours are called SYMBOLS. On maps, symbols are words, colours or drawings that stand for parts of the real world.

Activity 2:2

(a) (i) Draw and label a selection of symbols used by television weather forecasters on their maps.
(ii) Draw and name a selection of road signs which use symbols to tell you about road conditions and situations.

(b) Make up symbols for other everyday objects. Test them on a partner to see how well they work. See if he or she understands your purpose.

(c) Make yourself a new timetable for your week at school. Design symbols for each activity and fit them into the correct spaces on your timetable. Compare your timetable with those of the other people in your class. See who has created symbols that are simple, direct and consistent.

Figure 2.1   An aerial photograph of part of South Devon

(d) In your home or school area, make a collection of other examples of symbols. Remember to find not only those symbols you see but also those you smell (such as freshly ground coffee which indicates a coffee shop), and those you hear (such as a police siren). For each symbol work out: who made it, why they made it, who it is designed for and where it is used.

In much the same way as your symbols represent everyday objects, the small grey and white patches on the photograph are symbols that also represent something. They stand for real fields that actually exist at this moment. The photograph is a kind of map, but how useful is it for finding places, or for finding your way around? Map 1 (pages 18–19) shows an accurate bird's eye view of part of South Devon. It is made by the ORDNANCE SURVEY, a British government organisation that makes many different sorts of maps of Britain. Perhaps, at first sight, you may have the same problem as Freddy (Figure 2.2)!

Key 1 For Maps 1,2,4 (1:2500) and 10 (1:1250)

SYMBOLS AND CONVENTIONAL SIGNS

⊶ ....Site of antiquity
⤚⟶ ....Direction of water flow
↑ B M ....Bench mark (normal)
↑ F B M ....Bench mark (fundamental)
⊗ ....Cave entrance
▣ ....Pylon
· ts ....Traverse station (permanent)
· rp ....Revision point (instrumentally fixed)
↑ rp ....Revision point & bench mark coincident
+ ....Surface level
△ ....Triangulation station
∫ ....Area brace (1:2500 scale only)
⸮ ....Limit of area within which individual
                                parcels are not shown

ABBREVIATIONS IN FREQUENT USE

B H .... Beer House
B P, B S ...Boundary Post, Boundary Stone
Cn, C ....Capstan, Crane
Chy.....................................Chimney
D Fn.....................Drinking Fountain
El P......................Electricity Pillar or Pole
E T L.......Electricity Transmission Line
F A P......................Fire Alarm Pillar
F S...Flagstaff
F B..................................Foot Bridge
F P.......................................Foot Path
G P....................................Guide Post
G V C......... Gas Valve Compound
H......................Hydrant or Hydraulic
L B......................................Letter Box
L C...............................Level Crossing
L Twr.........................Lighting Tower
L G..............................Loading Gauge
Meml..................................Memorial
M P U............................Mail Pick-up
M P.........Mile Post or Mooring Post
M S..Mile Stone
N T L.................Normal Tidal Limit
P......................Pillar, Pole or Post
Path (um).....................Unmade Path
P C.......................Public Convenience
P C B........................Police Call Box
P T P.............Police Telephone Pillar
P O.................................Post Office
P H................................Public House
Pp...Pump
S B, S Br........Signal Box, Signal Bridge
S P, S L...........Signal Post, Signal Light
Spr...Spring
S, S D.........................Stone, Sundial
Tk...............................Tank or Track
T C B....................Telephone Call Box
T C P.................Telephone Call Post
Tr..Trough
Wr Pt, Wr T...Water Point, Water Tap
W B.................................Weighbridge
W..Well
Wd Pp.........................Wind Pump

VEGETATION

.....................Bracken/Rough Grassland
.....................Coppice, Osier
.....................Heath
.....................Marsh, Saltings
.....................Reeds

ß ℧ ....Scrub
............................Non-coniferous trees
............................Coniferous trees
............................Surveyed trees
............................Orchard trees

The following vegetation symbols and categories used under previous specifications may appear on some maps

.....................Bracken/Rough Grassland
℧ ....Bush
.....................Coppice
.....................Furze

.....................Osier
....Rough Pasture
ß ℧ ℧ ....Scrub
℧ ℧ ℧ ....Underwood

Roofed Buildings		Greenhouses		Archways	Top	Slopes
1:1250	1:2500	1:1250	1:2500			
Culvert		Sloping Wall Top		Cliff Face / Cliff Metric maps only	Quarry Chalk Pit or Clay Pit	Rock Imperial maps only
Dunes		Sand		Shingle	Boulders Annotation only on metric maps below M H W	Rock Metric maps only Annotation only below M H W

Shown by annotation only on metric maps

Walls, other than those of roofed buildings, which are less than 1 metre thick at 1:1250 scale or 2 metres thick at 1:2500 scale, are shown by a single line representing the centre of the wall. Walls which are in excess of these widths are shown by two lines, each representing one face. For roofed buildings, the lines on the map normally represent the outer face of the walls at ground level.

Thick Wall   Thin Walls   Represented by
Building

BOUNDARY INFORMATION

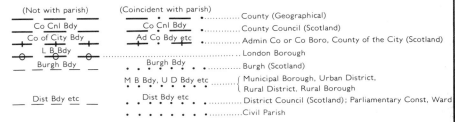

ENGLAND AND WALES   SCOTLAND

County .... Region or Islands Area
District..District
London Borough..
Civil Parish (England) }
Community (Wales) }
Electoral Division.............................. E D Bdy ....Electoral Division
Ward..................................... Ward Bdy ....Ward
Constituency (County Borough .... Boro Const Bdy   Burgh Const Bdy ....Constituency (County, Burgh
      or European Assembly)   Euro Const Bdy   Co Const Bdy   or European Assembly)
                                                              Boro Const & E D Bdy

Coincident boundaries are shown by the first appropriate symbol above, e.g. •━━━━━━━•
For Ordnance Survey purposes County Boundary is deemed to be the limit of the parish structure whether or not a parish area adjoins

On maps prior to Local Government reorganisation in England and Wales (April 1974) and in Scotland (May 1975) shown as below

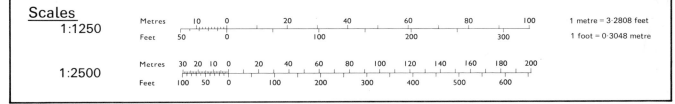

(Not with parish)	(Coincident with parish)	
Co Cnl Bdy	Co Cnl Bdy	County (Geographical)
Co of City Bdy	Ad Co Bdy etc	County Council (Scotland)
L B Bdy		Admin Co or Co Boro, County of the City (Scotland)
Burgh Bdy	Burgh Bdy	London Borough
	M B Bdy, U D Bdy etc	Burgh (Scotland)
		{ Municipal Borough, Urban District, Rural District, Rural Borough
Dist Bdy etc	Dist Bdy etc	District Council (Scotland); Parliamentary Const, Ward
		Civil Parish

Levelling Information: Altitudes of bench marks and surface levels are given in feet above the Newlyn Datum on maps published prior to Oct 1969 and in metres on maps published since that date. Bench Mark Lists, which may contain later levelling information, are obtainable from the Ordnance Survey, Southampton.

Scales

1:1250

Metres 10 0 20 40 60 80 100
Feet 50 0 100 200 300

1 metre = 3·2808 feet
1 foot = 0·3048 metre

1:2500

Metres 30 20 10 0 20 40 60 80 100 120 140 160 180 200
Feet 100 50 0 100 200 300 400 500 600

Map 1 Shinner's Bridge (1:2500)

Map 1

▲ Figure 2.2   Freddy's problem

Activity 2:3

(a) Sketch your own cartoon showing Freddy in another situation that has resulted from his inability to understand map symbols.

(b) Write a humorous short story about a would-be tourist guide, Ivor M. Lost, who starts a new job with Hopeful Tours Ltd. His first coach trip is to France, Belgium and Holland. His first problem is reading the maps, but he will not admit that he does not understand the symbols! Freddy and Ivor should be told that it takes only a short while to learn the new map language needed to read a map.

Activity 2:4

(a) Let your fingers do the walking! Put your finger on Lownard on Map 1. Follow the *footpath* between the *orchard* and the *woodland* towards the *Playing Field*. Carry on till you get to the *bench mark* 72.06 (a point where the height has been accurately measured). Run your finger down the B3372 *road* to the *Post Office* opposite the *School* and turn left at the *crossroads*. Some way past the *Electricity Sub Station* a *footpath* joins the road, on your right. Turn to your left and, with Lownard in front of you (in the distance) jump

your finger over the *fence* into the *field*. Cross the field to the *footbridge* over the *Bidwell Brook*. Keeping in the same direction, head back to the original footpath and retrace the beginning of your walk to Lownard.

(b) How much difficulty did you have following this route? What features could you not find?

(c) Devise a walk from Broom Park Estate and give your partner a list of instructions for him or her to follow the walk with their finger on the map. Did your partner end up where you intended? If the answer is 'no', then try again.

Possibly without realising it, the last activities have shown you that you already recognise a number of map symbols. You are now well on the way to understanding map language. A MAP SYMBOL is the general name given to all the dots, lines, patches, words and numbers on a map, that Freddy and Ivor found so confusing. Key 1, on page 17, is a list of the main symbols (and their meanings) that are used on the 1:2500 map. This list is called a KEY. It will unlock the mysteries of the Ordnance Survey map for you.

Activity 2:5

(a) On Map 1 find the square containing the words 'Youth Hostel'. Make a list of all the symbols in that square and find out what each one means.

(b) Carefully trace the drawings shown in Figure 2.3. They are parts of symbols that have not been fully drawn. Place your tracing over the map and complete the drawings by finding the correct symbol and matching it with your traced lines. Label the completed tracing.

(c) To play the Select-a-Square Game, you need ten pieces of paper cut into four-by-four-centimetre squares. Below are written descriptions of the symbols to be found inside ten different squares on the map (Map 1). You have to identify which square is being described in each case and cover that square with one of the pieces of paper. When the ten squares have been covered they form a letter of the alphabet. Which one will it be?
(i) Square one contains part of a playing field, footpath, field boundaries, LAND PARCEL NUMBER

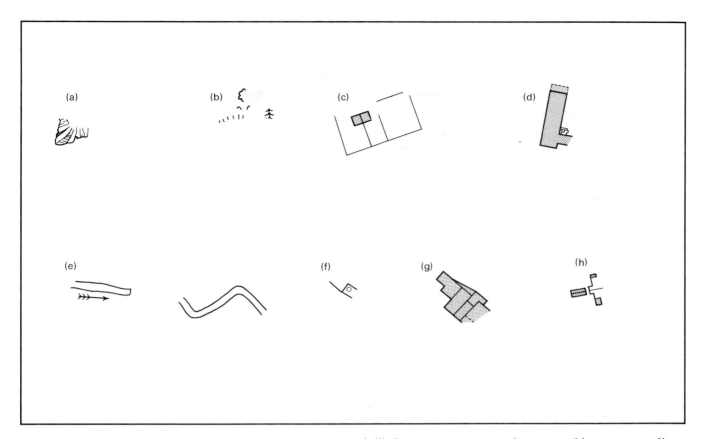

▲ Figure 2.3   Incomplete symbols from the OS 1:2500 map

(i.e. the number given to each section or parcel of land shown on the map), AREA NUMBER (i.e. the area of the land parcel in acres, as calculated by the Ordnance Survey), and a tiny section of orchard.

(ii) Square two contains a footpath with its land parcel number and area number shown, and a stream or drain.

(iii) Square three contains a stream with an arrow to show direction of flow. The stream is crossed by a footbridge. There is a name, two land parcel numbers and area numbers, a field boundary and an AREA BRACE (i.e. an 'S' shape that links two patches of land into one land parcel for the purposes of measurement).

(iv) Square four contains a garage, orchard, most of a large building, boundary lines, a footpath and a small section of the B3372 road.

(v) Square five contains only a road, and an area number.

(vi) Square six contains apparently nothing! However, there is just one field boundary, probably a hedge, running close to one edge of the square.

(vii) Square seven contains several houses, small orchards, road, track, water pump, several land parcel numbers and area numbers, area braces and a village hall.

(viii) Square eight contains a road with just its area number, and a land parcel number with its associated area number.

(ix) Square nine contains part of a road, a stream, a drain with an arrow showing direction of flow, some non-coniferous trees, a large building, an area brace, a land parcel number and an area number.

(x) Square ten contains part of the B3372, a BENCH MARK (i.e. a point where the height has been accurately measured), saw mill, travelling crane, private roads, orchard, two land parcel numbers, area numbers and several area braces.

(d) (i) Look again at square six, which apparently contained nothing. Do not be fooled! What do you think is there besides the hedge, but has not been marked on the map?

(ii) Find other blank spaces on the map, like those around the houses at Broom Park Estate. How are these blank spaces used?

(iii) Give reasons why the Ordnance Survey has not devised symbols for these uses.

Keeping your distance

We are all familiar with the distances that we travel regularly. For example, you are familiar with the distance from your home to your school, but what about the distance between places that you have never been to? In the following activity, you will meet both familiar and unfamiliar distances.

Activity 2:6

(a) Rank the places (i) to (vi) in the order of their distance from the point where you are sitting at the moment. (The shortest distance will be number one and the longest distance will be number six. You do not need to know, or to write down, the exact distances.)
(i) Your home
(ii) The Headmaster's office
(iii) Rome
(iv) New York
(v) The centre of London
(vi) Paris

(b) Suggest two distances that are shorter than the shortest distance and two that are longer than the longest.

RELATIVE DISTANCES, such as those above, are often easier to judge than ABSOLUTE DISTANCES, which have exact lengths. You have already learned, in Chapter 1, that distance can be measured in paces. However, this is rather imprecise because not everybody's pace is the same length.

Activity 2:7

(a) What other ways are there for measuring horizontal distance on the ground?

(b) Which method would be best for measuring: your desk top; a kitchen that is being fitted with cupboards; a school boy's practice long jump; a javelin throw that is close to the world record; the distance between two petrol filling stations, to work out a car's petrol consumption; the distance between Paris and Milan, to work out the approximate time of arrival of a long-distance coach trip? Justify your choice of method of measurement in each case.

One unit of measurement that, unlike the pace length, is the same the whole world over, is the metre. If you are unfamiliar with this distance, measure out a metre on the floor next to your desk.

On the map (Map 1) the representation of one metre is very small. In fact, just one millimetre on the map represents two and a half metres on the ground. Study the border of the map and you will notice that it is divided into small blocks. Each block stands for ten metres on the ground. Do you know the size of your classroom? Find a building on the map that would be about the same size as your classroom if it was drawn at the same scale as the map. In answering Activity 2:7, did you suggest that a map might be used to calculate distance? Sometimes a map can save time and effort. For example, workers laying a pipe or installing telephone lines might like to measure distance on a map. In this way they could assess likely costs before making detailed measurements on the ground.

The technique for map measurement is quite simple. First, use a piece of paper with a straight edge. Place it on the map so that the edge of it passes through the small cross labelled 49 in the centre of Shinner's Bridge crossroads, and the small cross labelled 45, nearby. Second, mark each place with a line on the paper's edge and then hold the paper's edge along the border of the map. Third, count up the number of blocks along the border that fall between your two lines to get a rough measurement (remembering that each block represents ten metres). If your marks do not match with an exact number of blocks, use the blocks in the corners of the map border, which have been subdivided into representations of individual metres. In the Shinner's Bridge example, the distance is about 58 metres.

Activity 2:8

(a) Suppose the Shinner's Bridge crossroads has become an accident black spot. Why might the crossroads be dangerous for both cars and pedestrians? How could it be made safer?

(b) Since many accidents to pedestrians occur at night, imagine the local people want to have street lighting put in along the four roads leading from Shinner's Bridge crossroads. Your job is to make a rough estimate of costs. The instructions are as follows:

(i) Costs for digging a trench and laying an electricity supply line are £50 per 10 metres. Each lamp-post costs £100 and they need to be approximately 30 metres apart.

(ii) Your layout design should take the form of a straight line from the electricity sub station near Shinner's Bridge Farm, to the centre of the crossroads. From there, three other straight lines should be laid along the other roads. Lay one line down the B3372 as far as the bench mark (72.06). Lay another line past the Village Hall to the edge of the map. Lastly, lay another line as far as the guide post along the road going to the right.

(iii) First, trace the road outline. Second, add the lines of the four buried electricity cables and measure their total length. Third, position lamp-posts at suitable points on your tracing on alternate sides of the road. Bear in mind the parts of the road that need most light. Fourth, draw lines to represent buried cable from the centre line to each lamp-post. Add up the total extra length of cable needed and find out your total costs.

In the last activity you measured several STRAIGHT LINE DISTANCES. In fact, you can see that these lines together make up a CROOKED DISTANCE. This shows you how easy it can be to measure crooked distances. As you have found, you simply break the crooked distance into straight sections and measure each section separately, adding it to the previous measurement. You use the straight edge of a piece of paper just as you did for the straight distance measurement. There should be no spaces between the marking of one section and the next. The total distance will be the distance between the first and last marks, which you calculate by using the border. For example, the distance from the spot height marked 45 at Shinner's Bridge, along the road to the bench mark (90.16) next to Shinner's Bridge Quarry, is about 128 metres (i.e. 26 + 23 + 23 + 56 = 128 metres).

Activity 2:9

(a) Plan a walk, titled 'The Jobs People Do', for the five- and six-year-old children at the Shinner's Bridge school. Remembering the title, choose relevant points from the map that you want them to visit and plot them on tracing paper. When you are working out the route, bear safety in mind. The route should not be more than one kilometre in length.

(b) Plan a second walk, titled 'A Nature Walk in the Shinner's Bridge Area', for eight- and nine-year-old children at the school. Choose suitable places for them to study such habitats as farmland, different types of woodland, scrubland, rough grassland, and fresh water. When you trace and measure a route, remember that they are allowed to cross fields, but must beware of road dangers. Two kilometres is the maximum distance of the walk.

(c) Lastly, in this section devoted to distance, find the guide post at Shinner's Bridge crossroads. Think what it must look like and then draw the road sign that points along the B3372. Study the map carefully to find the city that appears on the sign and the distance shown. This road sign suggests that very often we need to know direction as well as distance.

Where do we go from here?

Where is your classroom door? Where is your teacher? Where are the windows? These are easy questions to answer. It gets more difficult if you try to point at things out of sight. How good is your SENSE OF DIRECTION? Your whole class could try to point towards the main school entrance, the Headmaster's office, the staffroom. If you all point at the same time, it can be revealing. How many people got the directions right? Try to point to other places in your local area. Your teacher will tell you the exact directions. More difficult still, try pointing towards places in other parts of the world. Do some people have a better sense of direction than others? Actually, a sense of direction is not born with us. Having a sense of direction is being able to spot clues in the environment, or surroundings, and using those clues to guide you. One set of clues we often use is LANDMARKS. These are distinctive, natural or artificial features in the landscape.

Activity 2:10

(a) What are the most important landmarks in your home area? List six and compare the list with the other people in your class.

(b) You may have read some of the many exciting stories that have been written about getting lost and finding the way back home. In one such story called *The Weirdstone of Brisingamen*, by Alan Garner, two children, Colin and Sue, were being chased by the evil Maggot-breed of Ymir through a beech wood. Read the following extract:

'Stop Sue!' yelled Colin.
He realised that their only hope of escape lay in reaching open ground and the path that led from Stormy Point to the road, where their longer legs might outdistance their pursuers', and even that seemed a slim chance.
'Stop Sue! We must . . . not go . . . down . . . any further! Find Stormy Point . . . somehow!'

All the while he was looking for a recognisable landmark, since in the fear and dusk he had lost his bearings, and all he knew was that their way lay uphill and not down.
Then, through the trees, he saw what he needed. About a hundred feet above them and to their right a tooth-shaped boulder stood against the sky: its distinctive shape had caught his eye when they had walked past it along a track coming from Stormy Point!
'That boulder! Make for that boulder!'

(i) What was Colin's and Sue's only hope of escape?
(ii) How had they lost their way?
(iii) There were only two things that Colin knew would help them to find their way. What were they?

(c) If you took a walk in the countryside, what are the landmarks that you would observe to help you find your way home if you got lost?

(d) What are the problems involved in using landmarks alone to find your way?

There are other clues in the environment to look for. NATURE'S SIGNPOSTS tell us directions, too. You have probably met the terms north, east, south and west.

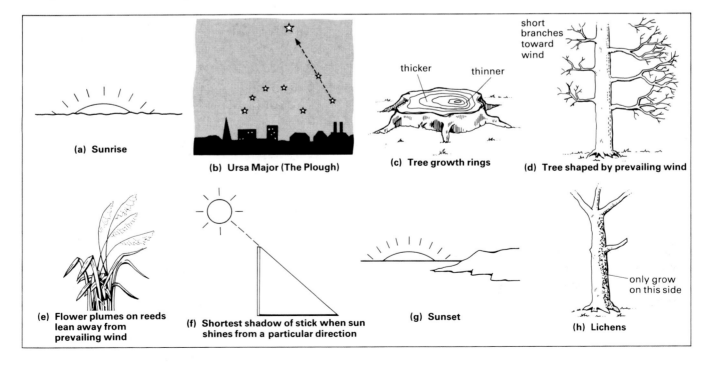

(a) Sunrise

(b) Ursa Major (The Plough)

(c) Tree growth rings — thicker, thinner

(d) Tree shaped by prevailing wind — short branches toward wind

(e) Flower plumes on reeds lean away from prevailing wind

(f) Shortest shadow of stick when sun shines from a particular direction

(g) Sunset

(h) Lichens — only grow on this side

▲ Figure 2.4   Nature's signposts

Activity 2:11

(a) Study Figure 2.4, which shows eight sketches of nature's signposts. Discuss for a few minutes, in small groups, what direction each feature might show if you saw them near your school. If you cannot decide directions for all of them, use your initiative to find the answers, or perhaps your teacher will tell you the correct answers later.

(b) Comment on the reliability of nature's signposts. Which ones would you trust the most and which the least?

(c) Try to find and sketch examples of these natural indicators in your home area.

(d) (i) Sketch examples of man-made indicators in the same area.
(ii) How do the man-made ones compare with the natural signposts in accuracy?

There is another very important natural signpost: the earthly magnet. The earth's core is iron, which acts like a giant magnet. You can test how it works by floating a magnetised needle on water. The earth's magnetic force draws it round to point north. This is exactly what happens in most compasses. Ask your teacher for a compass and use it to find north. Cut out a paper arrow and place it on your desk, pointing north. Using paper signs, your class can label the classroom walls with the appropriate names of the points of the compass. You may need to use Figure 2.5, a COMPASS ROSE, which labels eight major directions.

Turn back to Map 1. You can use this direction-finding system on the map. The direction to the top edge of the map is north. Knowing this information, you will see that Woodcott is at the west edge and the B3372 road disappears off the south edge.

Activity 2:12

(a) Use tracing paper to copy Figure 2.5. Place your compass rose over the Shinner's Bridge crossroads and state the rough direction of the roads from the crossroads to the edges of the map.

(b) Place the compass rose over the school and say the directions from the school to: Shinner's Bridge Farm, Broom Park Estate, the Raingauge, and the quarry at Lownard.

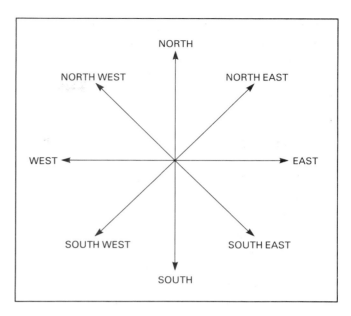

▲ Figure 2.5   Eight point compass rose

(c) State the major directions followed by someone walking from the Post Office to Lownard along the footpath.

Activity 2:13

(a) A small group of older children at the school have a secret camp. It can only be found by cracking a code that involves both distance and direction. The code is:

    school gate . . . NE 70 . . . SE 30 . . . E45 . . . N30 . . . NE 45 . . . E50 . . . N60 . . . secret camp.

(i) Find the camp.
(ii) Use the code to construct your own directions from the school to a secret hiding place of your choice on the map.

(b) Find the following places using the direction riddles below:
(i) I am south of the school, west of the Almshouses and south-east of the smaller Playing Field. Where am I?
(ii) I am north-west of the Raingauge, west of the Old Quarry and north of Lownard. Where am I?
(iii) I am north-west of Shinner's Bridge crossroads, east of the Youth Hostel and west of the Electricity Sub Station. Where am I?

(c) Compose similar direction riddles and try them on your neighbour.

Map 2 Shinner's Bridge (1:2500)

Map 2

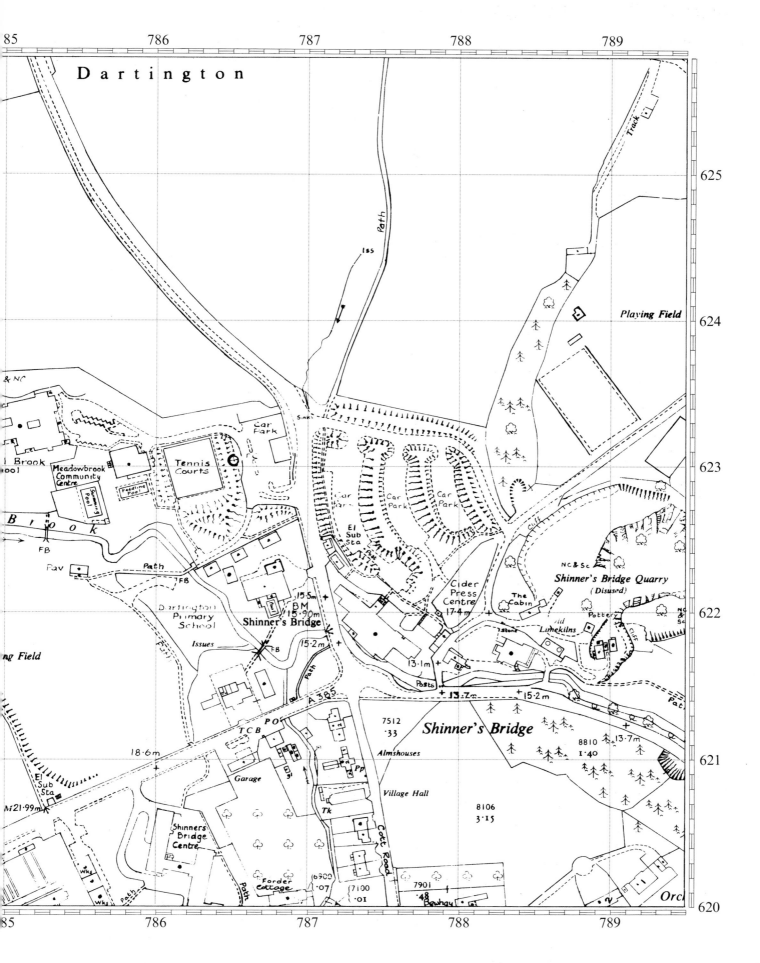

Dartington

Playing Field

Shinner's Bridge Quarry
(Disused)

Cider
Press
Centre

Shinner's Bridge

Meadowbrook
Community
Centre

Tennis
Courts

Dartington
Primary
School

Car Park

Shinners
Bridge
Centre

Almshouses

Village Hall

Forder
Cottage

Activity 2:14

(a) Try to work out which way the photograph, Figure 2.1, was taken. In this activity it might be easiest to work in pairs, using two books. Turn the map, Map 1, around until the features on the map match those in the photograph. Although much of the photograph falls off the map, there are enough signs, such as the Garage, School and Village Hall, to tell you the direction the photographer was facing. This is called ORIENTING A MAP or SETTING A MAP, and it is something you should try to do whenever you use a map.

Maps and time

As you may have realised from 'A moment in time' in Chapter 1, maps and photographs capture the landscape at an instant in time. But, the landscape around Shinner's Bridge has changed a great deal over the years.

Activity 2:15

As you read the following account, try to identify the features on Figure 2.1 and Map 1.

Before the 1920s, the landscape had been devoted to farming. This farming pattern of small farms like Lownard and Shinner's Bridge Farms had become established over hundreds of years. They concentrated on dairy and cereal products, along with apples for cider, all for local use. The fields were small, surrounded by high hedges with clumps of woodland here and there. The old quarries were worked for building stone, or to quarry limestone, which was burnt in the limekilns for lime to spread on the fields. The school and almshouse had also been built before 1920.

From 1920 to 1953, farming land changed hands, with some farms getting bigger at the expense of smaller ones like Lownard Farm. The Shinner's Bridge farmer built a larger barn across the road from his existing buildings. The four small fields south-east of Lownard were made into one large orchard and some fields became playing fields. Electricity reached the area, and with it industry grew. The textile mill,

saw mill and pottery were built. The expanding local community built houses at Broom Park and at Shinner's Bridge and were helped by the building of a new garage, Post Office, and office building.

What has happened since 1953? The Ordnance Survey is well aware that maps go out-of-date and they are constantly revising their maps. It is not sensible, however, to redraw a map each time a house is built or a road widened. Therefore, they gather all the new information on a special document and redraw the map when a certain amount of change has taken place. The special documents are known as the MASTER SURVEY DRAWINGS (MSD) and part of the drawing for the Shinner's Bridge area is shown in Map 2 (pages 26–7).

Activity 2:16

(a) Study Map 2 carefully and note all the differences between it and Map 1. Write a brief history of the landscape of the Shinner's Bridge area from 1953 onwards, using this information. The photograph, Figure 2.1, provides some evidence of change in the 1950s, for it was taken in 1961.

(b) How satisfactory are maps and aerial photographs for recording landscape change? Think about the time between each map or photograph and what is shown on both of them.

CHAPTER 3

Dartington

Where it's at

I spy with my little eye, something which is near the blackboard, a long way from the door, but very close to the map chest. What is it?

Activity 3:1

(a) Take it in turns to describe the location of an object in your classroom. The first person to guess what the object is, gives the next 'I spy' description.

(b) 'I spy in my mind's eye . . .' Repeat the I spy game of Activity 3:1(a). This time, describe the location of an object that you know of somewhere in your local area. Choose one that you cannot see at the moment.

This section of Chapter 3 deals with the idea of LOCATION (i.e. the position of things on the earth's surface). The words you used in Activity 3:1 described the RELATIVE LOCATION of things. Why did you find some things easier to pinpoint than others? In some situations, there is a better way of describing location than relying on spoken descriptions. You could use a map.

Activity 3:2

(a) On a large, local O.S. map or sketch map on the wall, use a coloured pin, flag or label to pinpoint the place where you live. When the whole class has done this, think of words to describe the patterns shown. Then discuss, as a class group, possible reasons for the location patterns shown by the pins.

(b) There are other important places in the local area besides those marked in 3:2(a). Quickly list six places that you feel are important. Your teacher will now compile a short list of places that you, as a class, felt were important. Mark these on the map with a set of pins or labels that are a different colour from those used in 3:2(a). Can you think of reasons to explain the selection of places?

(c) Not only do people and places have locations, but so, too, do events.
(i) Moving from the local area to the whole of Britain, collect newspaper articles, over the next few days, about events in Britain that interest you. Number them and pin them to a bulletin board. To find where each event took place, study an atlas or wall map showing the names of places.

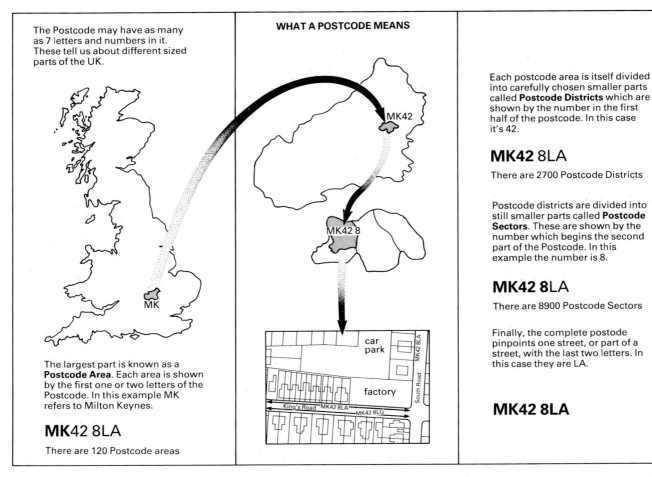

The Postcode may have as many as 7 letters and numbers in it. These tell us about different sized parts of the UK.

The largest part is known as a **Postcode Area**. Each area is shown by the first one or two letters of the Postcode. In this example MK refers to Milton Keynes.

MK42 8LA

There are 120 Postcode areas

WHAT A POSTCODE MEANS

Each postcode area is itself divided into carefully chosen smaller parts called **Postcode Districts** which are shown by the number in the first half of the postcode. In this case it's 42.

MK42 8LA

There are 2700 Postcode Districts

Postcode districts are divided into still smaller parts called **Postcode Sectors**. These are shown by the number which begins the second part of the Postcode. In this example the number is 8.

MK42 8LA

There are 8900 Postcode Sectors

Finally, the complete postode pinpoints one street, or part of a street, with the last two letters. In this case they are LA.

MK42 8LA

▲ Figure 3.1   The Postcode system

Why is it easier to find some places than others? With the help of your teacher, locate the place names that you missed on your first attempt. On a large outline wall map of Britain, put the number of each article in its correct place. The wallmap and bulletin board can be titled 'News Over Britain'.

(ii) Discuss where most of the newsworthy events took place. Think of likely reasons for the location patterns shown.

(d) As you may have discovered, finding the location of places in Britain can be difficult and time-consuming. However, finding places is much easier if you have the fuller information that is contained in an address. Draw an envelope and address it to yourself as accurately as possible.

Millions of letters pass through the postal system in our country and the Post Office has been trying to ease the task of sorting out the letters. They have some machines to do this work. The machines need to be able to recognise immediately the destination of each letter. That is why the Post Office has introduced the Postcode. Did you include the Postcode on your envelope? It is a sort of shorthand address, containing all the information for the machine to do its job. The way the Postcode system works is shown in Figure 3.1.

Activity 3:3

(a) (i) Write the Postcode for your home or school address in large letters and numbers. Study Figure 3.1 and use four different colours for the four different parts of the code.
(ii) Label the first three parts: Postcode Area; Postcode District; Postcode Sector.
(iii) Although it is always best to write an address in full, it is possible to get a letter delivered with the Postcode and one other piece of information. What is that information?

(b) Explain possible benefits and problems of the whole Postcode System to the public and to postal workers.

The Postcode System is a way of referring to the location of a specific place (i.e. its ABSOLUTE LOCATION). There are many other methods in use that do the same thing. For example, what systems are used in cinemas and sports stadiums to locate seats? How are the classrooms numbered in your school? How well do these ways of locating places work?

Frequently, the GRID SYSTEM is used to locate things on maps, and the following activity will teach you how to use it.

Activity 3:4

The object of the Space Race game is for you to colonise an asteroid that has valuable minerals. It is a race between two galactic mining companies. Each company needs to put together sufficient men and materials to be able to claim, under intergalactic law, the total mineral rights of the asteroid.

(i) It is played on a large blackboard or wall sketch map of an imaginary asteroid called 'O.S.381', which has a fairly flat side where the minerals are found. On the map is drawn a grid of eleven lines. The lines are numbered from 00 to 10 up the grid and from 00 to 10 from left to right across the grid.

(ii) The class is divided into two teams, or mineral companies, who land men and materials by spaceship on the asteroid. Each company takes it in turn to land a spaceship on the asteroid at any point where the grid lines cross. Each person in the company guides one spaceship to land by calling out the coordinates of the point (give the vertical line number first and the horizontal line number second) to your teacher. Your teacher will mark the landing, in your company's colour, on the map. Landings must be made strictly in turn in an order decided by your teacher.

(iii) The company that gains the mineral rights is the one that gets five spaceships landed in a line. This can be either a horizontal, vertical or diagonal line. Be on the lookout to create a run of five in a line for the next person in your company, as well as stopping the other company setting up their own line of five.

Back on planet Earth, the Ordnance Survey use a GRID REFERENCE SYSTEM, too! The O.S.1:10 560 map extract of Dartington, South Devon is shown in Map 3 (page 38). The grid lines numbered 78, 79 and 80, running up and down the map, are called EASTINGS. The grid lines numbered 62 and 63, running across the map, are called NORTHINGS.

To refer to a specific grid square, look at the southwest (lower left) corner of the square, and name the easting and northing that cross at that point. The easting number should always be written first and it should be followed by the northing number. For instance, Shinner's Bridge is in square 78 62. In which square do you find North Wood? What is the four-figure grid reference for the square containing Week?

The grid for Map 3 has been drawn in outline on Figure 3.2. The hamlet, Lownard, is in a square between eastings 78 and 79. The border between them is divided into tenths. Lownard lies two-tenths of the distance from easting 78, so it is located on easting 782.

The same square, containing Lownard, is also between lines 62 and 63 and, again, the border is divided into tenths. This time, Lownard lies two-tenths north of northing 62, so it is located on northing 622.

Put the easting number and the northing number together and you get a SIX-FIGURE GRID REFERENCE NUMBER, 782 622, which locates Lownard on the map. Remember that you always write the easting number first, and then write the northing number.

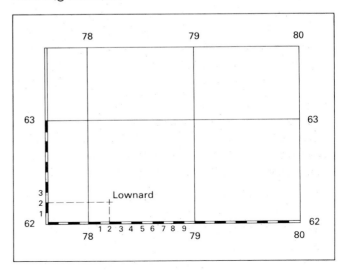

▲ Figure 3.2   Six-figure grid reference

At this stage, it may help to cut out a piece of tracing paper that is slightly larger than a grid square on Map 3. Draw the square and then add further lines across and up and down the traced grid square to show the position of the tenths. This can then be placed over any grid square to help you to locate any point on the map.

Sometimes the place does not fall exactly under a point where any lines cross. If this is the case, you give the grid reference of the nearest crossing point of lines to the south west. For example, the grid reference of Saint Mary's Church is 785 626.

Activity 3:5

(a) Using Map 3, rewrite the six-figure grid references for the following places, adding the missing figures:
(i) The word 'Broom' 78 __ 62 __
(ii) Shinner's Bridge crossroads 78 __ __ __ __
(iii) The nursery at Symon's Tree Barn 79 __ __ __ __ __
(iv) The centre of Chacegrove Wood __ __ __ __ __ __

(b) What things can be found at the following six-figure grid references? You may need to use Key 2A, on page 35, to help identify them.
(i) 785 620
(ii) 781 631
(iii) 780 629
(iv) 797 620.

Activity 3:6

It is possible to pinpoint places with even more accuracy.
(a) On a traced grid, like the one described just before Activity 3:5, measure the side of one of the small squares that has been formed by the tenths lines. Use the scale shown in the key, Key 2A, to calculate the actual ground distance represented by this one side.

(b) (i) From Activity 3:6(a), it is obvious that even one of the small squares covers a large area of land. Think of how you would pinpoint a place with more accuracy within this square.
(ii) Write an eight-figure grid reference for the 'n' in Lownard on the map.

(iii) Think of reasons why the Ordnance Survey does not print all the extra grid lines on the map to make grid references even easier to work out.

John Holand, a nobleman who was a half-brother to Richard II, built Dartington Hall in the years following 1384. But John got into trouble with King Richard and at one time was in danger of losing all his money and lands. Suppose that, to guard against this, he secretly buried several valuable objects in the land around Dartington Hall (798 627). You now have a chance to hunt for the treasure in the game that follows. The rules are explained in Activity 3:7.

Activity 3:7

(a) This Treasure Hunt game is for two players. The first player takes the role of John Holand, who buries treasure in the grid square 79 62. The second player takes the role of a modern treasure hunter who searches for the treasure with a metal detector.

(b) The object of the game is for the treasure hunter to discover as much treasure as possible. Then the roles are reversed and the first player searches for treasure hidden by the second player. The one with the most treasure points wins the game.
(c) Each person should draw two grid squares on tracing paper. Add the lines for tenths, as explained before Activity 3:5. The first player, acting as John Holand, uses one traced grid to mark where he buries the treasure. Think carefully about locations that John Holand might choose when you are marking the hiding places. In other words, do not bury treasure in the middle of a field but choose hedgerows, or points near buildings or places in the woods. The treasure to be buried is: one jewelled crown (C), worth 20 points; three golden goblets (G), worth 5 points each; ten bags of money (M), worth 2 points each. Do not put more than one item of treasure in each small square.

(d) The treasure hunter has four 'days' to search for treasure. He or she can search five small squares each day. So, the treasure hunter calls out five six-figure grid references for each day of searching, marking each one on his/her own Treasure Hunt Grid as he/she calls them out. The player acting as John Holand marks them on his Buried Treasure Grid. At the end of each 'day', he tells the treasure hunter which of these squares, if any, contained some treasure.

Higher and higher

Photographs from spaceships show the world to be a sphere with a smooth surface. But the closer you get to it, the more lumpy the land surface appears. Actually living on the surface as we do, some parts seem to us to be very uneven indeed. Where are the highest parts of the world and where are the lowest?

Activity 3:8

(a) Try to rank the following things in order of their height. Put the highest at number one in your list and the lowest at number eight.
(i)   A double-decker bus
(ii)   The Empire State Building
(iii)   The chair you are sitting on
(iv)   Your teacher
(v)   Mount Everest
(vi)   Yourself
(vii)   A fully grown giraffe
(viii) The tallest building in your local town or city.

(b) This simple exercise shows you the idea of RELATIVE HEIGHTS. Choose three more things of different heights and add them, at the appropriate points, to your list.

Do you know how high the school playground is above sea level? Make a rough guess. When we are talking about the height of the school playground or of the land in general, we refer to its height above sea level. But the level of the sea is always changing. Thousands of years ago, when much of the world was in an ice age, water was trapped on the land as ice. This meant that the sea level was lower. As the temperature slowly rose, the ice melted. With more water around, the level of water in the sea began to rise.

Activity 3:9

If the present ice caps, especially those in Antarctica and Greenland, were to begin melting, what would happen? Name some places in Britain that might be flooded by the sea. Name some other places that would be very safe from the flooding sea.

The part of Devon shown on Map 3 is not very high above sea level. In fact, if the sea rose 50 feet (i.e. the height of, say, three double-decker buses piled on top of one another), the tide would cover the crossroads at Shinner's Bridge and the nearby garage might start repairing boats instead of cars! How does the symbol at the centre of the crossroads show that it could be flooded? Use Key 2A for help.

Activity 3:10

(a) Imagine what would happen to this part of Devon if the sea level rose to 250 feet above its present level. Study Map 3 carefully and find all the SPOT HEIGHTS that are higher than 250 feet. These heights have been accurately surveyed by the Ordnance Survey. Write down the six-figure grid references of the points and say how high each one is.

Dartington can be seen in the following sketches. Figure 3.3 shows the area flooded to the height of 250 feet above present sea level.

Activity 3:11

(a) How many islands can you see in the sketch? Was this number different from what you had expected? If so, why?

(b) A line has been drawn around the base of each island to show where a 'beach' would be formed. Let us call this *Sea Level One*. Suppose the sea level dropped 50 feet, to leave a new beach around the islands, as shown in Figure 3.4.
(i) What changes are shown in Figure 3.4?
(ii) How high is the old beach now above this *Sea Level Two*?
(iii) Imagine if you were to walk on the beach at Sea Level Two around North Wood Island. Would you be going uphill or downhill?

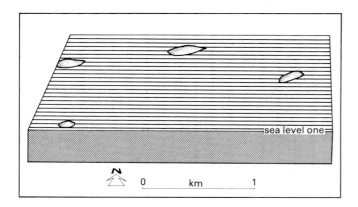

▲ Figure 3.3   Dartington, flooded up to 250 feet above present sea level

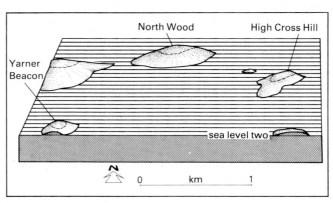

▲ Figure 3.4   Dartington, flooded up to 200 feet above present sea level

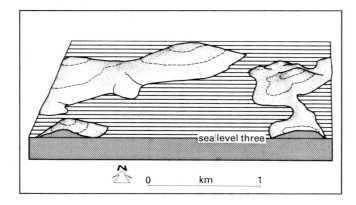

▲ Figure 3.5   Dartington, flooded up to 150 feet above present sea level

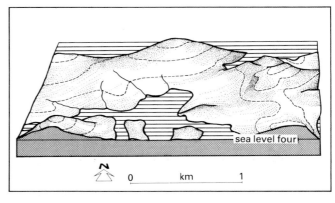

▲ Figure 3.6   Dartington, flooded up to 100 feet above present sea level

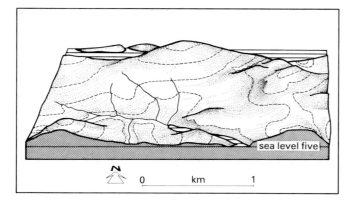

▲ Figure 3.7   Dartington, flooded up to 50 feet above present sea level

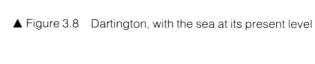

▲ Figure 3.8   Dartington, with the sea at its present level

Figure 3.5, 3.6, and 3.7 show the sea level dropping a further 50 feet each time. Each sea level has left a 'beach' behind, which marks its height. The last sketch, Figure 3.8, shows

Dartington with the sea at its present level, with all the beaches remaining. Each of these 'beach' lines join places at the same height above sea level.

Key 2A For Map 3 (1:10 560) and Map 12 (1:10 000)

ROADS

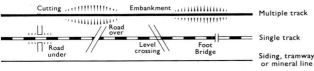

═══════ ┅┅┅┅ Road ═══Tk═══ ┅═══ Track ─ ─ ─ FP ─ ─ ─ Path

The representation on this map of a road, track or path is no evidence of the existence of a right of way

RAILWAYS

Cutting ·ıιιιιιιι Embankment ·ιιιιιιιιι Multiple track

Road over — Single track

Road under | Level crossing | Foot Bridge — Siding, tramway or mineral line

———————— Narrow gauge

GENERAL FEATURES

⊹	Antiquity (site of)		Chalk pit, clay pit or quarry
∘∘∘	Boulders (isolated or coastal)		Gravel pit
▣ ◼	Building; important building		Sand pit
⊠	Glasshouse		Refuse or slag heap
Pylon □ Pole •	Electricity transmission line		Sand
		∘∘∘	Shingle
△	Triangulation station		Sloping wall
⟶	Direction of flow of water		Lake, loch or pond

· · · · · · · · · Civil Parish Boundary (England), Community Boundary (Wales)

VEGETATION

1:10 000

⋀⋀⋀	Coniferous trees
⌒⌒⌒	Non-coniferous trees
⥾	Bracken
͵ͺ͵ͺ	Rough grassland
∩∩—	Scrub
͵ͺ͵	Heath

1:10 560

∴∴∵	Rough Pasture
∘∘∘	Bushes
⚊⚊	Marsh
∘∘∘	Underwood
∘∘∘	Orchard
⋀⋀	Coniferous trees
⌒⌒	Non-coniferous trees

ABBREVIATIONS

NTL	Normal Tidal Limit	PH	Public House
BP, BS	Boundary Post, Boundary Stone	MP, MS	Mile Post, Mile Stone
FB	Foot Bridge	PO	Post Office
GP	Guide Post	W	Well

ROCK FEATURES

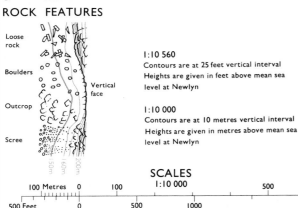

Loose rock
Boulders
Vertical face
Outcrop
Scree
50m 160m 200m

1:10 560
Contours are at 25 feet vertical interval
Heights are given in feet above mean sea level at Newlyn

1:10 000
Contours are at 10 metres vertical interval
Heights are given in metres above mean sea level at Newlyn

SCALES

1:10 000

100 Metres 0 100 500
500 Feet 0 500 1000 2000

1:10 560

100 Metres 0 100 500
500 Feet 0 500 1000 2000

Key 2B For Map 8 (1:250 000)

ROADS
Not necessarily rights of way

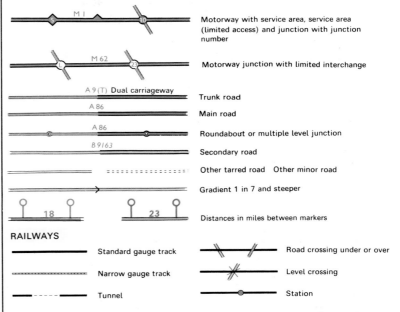

M 1 — Motorway with service area, service area (limited access) and junction with junction number

M 62 — Motorway junction with limited interchange

A 9 (T) Dual carriageway — Trunk road

A 86 — Main road

A 86 — Roundabout or multiple level junction

B 9163 — Secondary road

Other tarred road   Other minor road

⟶ Gradient 1 in 7 and steeper

18   23 — Distances in miles between markers

RAILWAYS

━━━━	Standard gauge track	⫻	Road crossing under or over
┅┅┅	Narrow gauge track	⤬	Level crossing
━ ─ ─	Tunnel	●━	Station

GENERAL FEATURES

. T . A . R	Telephone call box	PO AA RAC
	Buildings	
	Wood	
CANOVIVM ·	Roman antiquity	
Castle ·	Other antiquities	

⊕	Civil aerodrome
⩘	Lighthouse
▲	Youth hostel
ⵕ	Windmill
ⵉ	Radio or TV mast

WATER FEATURES

———————— Canal

Marsh

BOUNDARIES

⊢⊣⊢⊣ National

─ · ─ · ─ County, Region or Islands Area

TOURIST INFORMATION

✝	Abbey, Cathedral, Priory
♒	Ancient Monument
⋀	Camp site
⌂	Caravan site
▦	Castle
ⵙ	Country park
▶	Golf course or links
⛪	Historic house
⛊	Information centre
☆	Other tourist feature
⛟	Preserved railway

ⵚ	Racecourse
▦	Zoo
▥	Museum

RELIEF

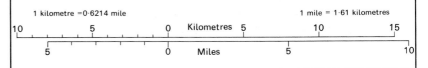

Feet	Metres
3000	914
2000	610
1400	427
1000	305
600	183
200	61
0	0

·274 Heights in feet above mean sea level

Contours at 200ft intervals

To convert feet to metres multiply by 0·3048

1 kilometre = 0·6214 mile   1 mile = 1·61 kilometres

10   5   0   Kilometres   5   10   15

5   0   Miles   5   10

Key 3 For Maps 5 and 9 (1:25 000)

Roads

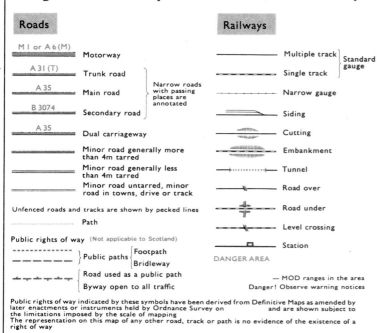

M1 or A6(M)	Motorway
A31(T)	Trunk road
A35	Main road
B3074	Secondary road

Narrow roads with passing places are annotated

A35 — Dual carriageway

Minor road generally more than 4m tarred

Minor road generally less than 4m tarred

Minor road untarred, minor road in towns, drive or track

Unfenced roads and tracks are shown by pecked lines

.... Path

Public rights of way (Not applicable to Scotland)

Public paths { Footpath / Bridleway

Road used as a public path

Byway open to all traffic

Public rights of way indicated by these symbols have been derived from Definitive Maps as amended by later enactments or instruments held by Ordnance Survey on   and are shown subject to the limitations imposed by the scale of mapping
The representation on this map of any other road, track or path is no evidence of the existence of a right of way

Railways

Multiple track	Standard gauge
Single track	
Narrow gauge	
Siding	
Cutting	
Embankment	
Tunnel	
Road over	
Road under	
Level crossing	
Station	

DANGER AREA

— MOD ranges in the area
Danger! Observe warning notices

Symbols

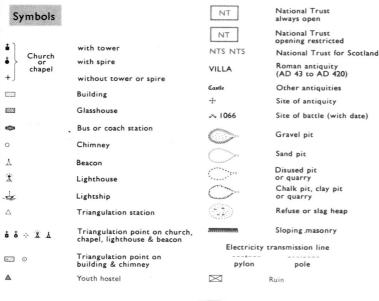

Church or chapel
- with tower
- with spire
- without tower or spire

Building

Glasshouse

Bus or coach station

Chimney

Beacon

Lighthouse

Lightship

Triangulation station

Triangulation point on church, chapel, lighthouse & beacon

Triangulation point on building & chimney

Youth hostel

NT	National Trust always open
NT	National Trust opening restricted
NTS NTS	National Trust for Scotland
VILLA	Roman antiquity (AD 43 to AD 420)
Castle	Other antiquities
	Site of antiquity
1066	Site of battle (with date)
	Gravel pit
	Sand pit
	Disused pit or quarry
	Chalk pit, clay pit or quarry
	Refuse or slag heap
	Sloping masonry

Electricity transmission line
- - - - pylon   pole

Ruin

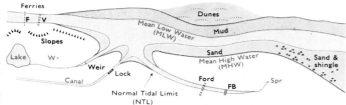

Ferries
F V
Dunes
Mean Low Water (MLW)
Mud
Slopes
Lake W
Sand
Mean High Water (MHW)
Sand & shingle
Weir
Canal
Lock
Ford
FB
Spr
Normal Tidal Limit (NTL)

Boundaries

.... { Civil Parish (England) / Community (Wales)
— — — — Constituency (Co, Boro or Burgh)

Rock Features

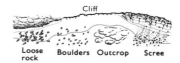

Cliff

Loose rock   Boulders   Outcrop   Scree

Heights

50· Determined by { ground survey
285·   { air survey

Surface heights are to the nearest metre above mean sea level. Heights shown close to a triangulation pillar refer to the station height at ground level and not necessarily to the summit

Map 9
Contours are at 10 metres vertical interval

Map 5
Contours have been surveyed at 25 feet vertical interval but values are given to the nearest metre

Vegetation

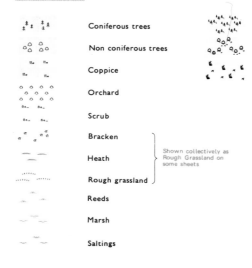

Coniferous trees	
Non coniferous trees	
Coppice	
Orchard	
Scrub	
Bracken	
Heath	Shown collectively as Rough Grassland on some sheets
Rough grassland	
Reeds	
Marsh	
Saltings	

Abbreviations

BP		Boundary Post
BS		Boundary Stone
Cemy		Cemetery
F Sta		Fire Station
FB		Foot Bridge
Hospl		Hospital
MP		Mile Post
MS		Mile Stone
Mon		Monument
P		Post office
Pol Sta	Rural areas only	Police Station
PC		Public Convenience
PH		Public House
Sch		School
Spr		Spring
T		Telephone, public
A		Telephone, AA
R		Telephone, RAC
TH		Town Hall
Twr		Tower
W		Well
Wd Pp		Wind Pump
Y		Youth hostel

Scale

Kilometres 1   0   1 Kilometres

Miles 1   ¾   ½   ¼   0   1 Miles

Key 4 For Maps 6,7 and 11(1:50 000)

ROADS AND PATHS **Not necessarily rights of way**

Junction number

Service area M 1   Elevated
Motorway (dual carriageway)

M 3
Motorway under construction

Unfenced   Footbridge
Trunk road
A 40 (T)
Dual carriageway
Main road

Main road under construction

B 284
Secondary road

A 855   Bridge   B 885
Narrow road with passing places

Road generally more than 4m wide

Road generally less than 4m wide

Other road, drive or track
Path
Gradient : 1 in 5 and steeper   1 in 7 to 1 in 5
Gates   Road tunnel

Ferry P   Ferry V
Ferry (passenger)   Ferry (vehicle)

PUBLIC RIGHTS OF WAY
(Not applicable to Scotland)

Footpath } Public paths
Bridleway

Road used as a public path
Byway open to all traffic

BOUNDARIES

National

London Borough

District

County, Region
or Islands Area

National Park
or Forest Park

FC   Forestry
Commission   Pedestrians only - observe local signs

WATER FEATURES

Marsh or salting
Towpath   Lock
Slopes   Cliff
High water mark
Flat rock
Low water mark
Aqueduct   Canal
Lighthouse (in use)
Ford
Weir   Sand   Dunes
Normal tidal limit
Lake   Bridge   Footbridge
Lighthouse (disused)   Beacon
Mud   Shingle
Canal (dry)

GENERAL FEATURES

Electricity transmission line
(with pylons spaced conventionally)

Pipe line
(arrow indicates direction of flow)

bruin   Buildings

Public buildings (selected)

Bus or coach station

Coniferous wood

Non-coniferous wood

Mixed wood

Orchard

Park or ornamental grounds

Quarry

Spoil heap, refuse tip or dump

Radio or TV mast

Church }
or { with tower
Chapel { with spire
without tower or spire

Chimney or tower

Glasshouse

Graticule intersection at 5' intervals

(H)   Heliport

△   Triangulation pillar

Windmill with or without sails

Windpump

RAILWAYS

Track multiple or single

Track narrow gauge

Freight line, siding or tramway

a   b   Station   (a) principal
(b) closed to passengers

LC   Level crossing

Embankment

Cutting

Bridges, Footbridge

Tunnel

Viaduct

dismtd rly   Dismantled railway line

ROCK FEATURES

outcrop
cliff
scree

HEIGHTS

76   Maps 6&11
Contour values are to the
nearest metre. The vertical
interval is, however, 50 feet

50   Map 7
Contours are at 10 metres
vertical interval

· 144   Heights are to the nearest
metre above mean sea level

TOURIST INFORMATION

Information centre   Caravan site

Parking   Public telephone

Picnic site   Motoring organisation telephone

View Point   Golf course or links

Camp site   Selected places of tourist interest

ABBREVIATIONS

Br	Bridge
Cemy	Cemetery
CG Sta	Coastguard Station
CH	Clubhouse
Chy	Chimney
Coll	College
Crem	Crematorium
El Sub Sta	Electricity Sub-Station
Fm	Farm
Ho	House
Hospl	Hospital
IRB Sta	Inshore Rescue Boat Station
LC	Level Crossing
MS	Milestone
Mus	Museum
P	Post Office
PC	Public convenience
PH	Public House
Sch	School
Sta	Station
TH	Town Hall, Guildhall or equivalent
Wks	Works
Wr Twr	Water tower

ANTIQUITIES

VILLA   Roman

Castle   Non-Roman

☆   Tumulus

𝔪   Ancient Monument

Kilometres

2   1   0   1   2

1   0   1

Miles

1 kilometre = 0·6214 mile

1 mile = 1·6093 kilometres

Map 3

Map 3 Dartington (1:10 560)

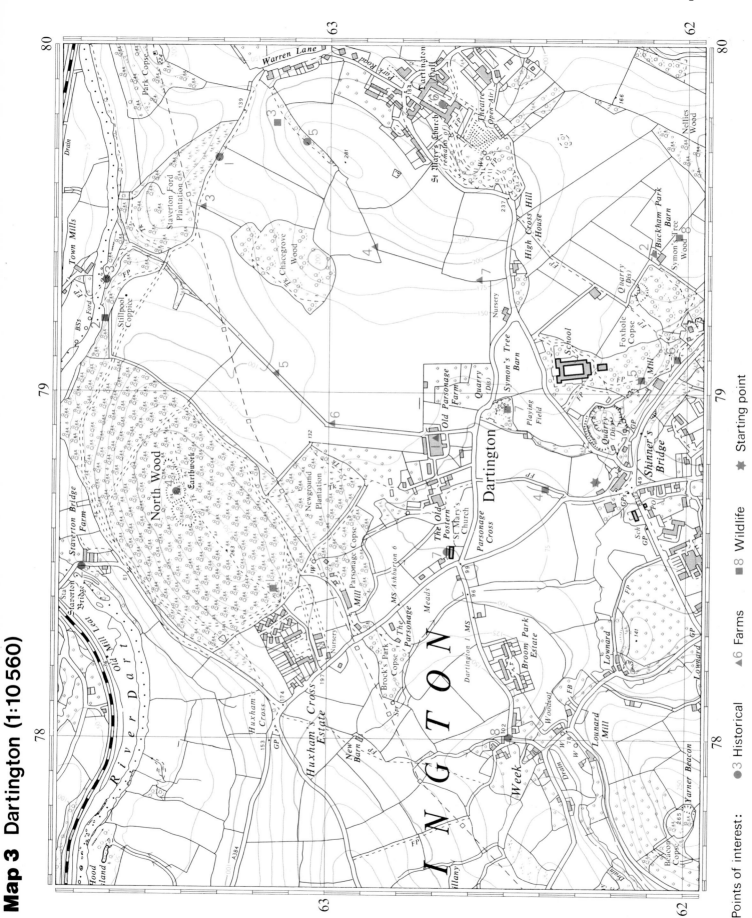

Activity 3:12

(a) Figure 3.9 shows a view of Dartington from directly overhead, with the sea at its present level. Compare it with Map 3. Name the symbol on the map that represents the sea level heights, shown by the 'beach' lines.

(b) A CONTOUR is a line that joins places that are the same height above sea level. It can be used, as well as spot heights, to tell us the elevation, or height, of places above sea level.

(i) What is the CONTOUR INTERVAL (i.e. the difference in height between each contour) on this map?

(ii) Most contours are numbered, but you may have to trace your finger along them till you find a number. For example, what are the heights of the contours running through Chacegrove Wood (794 631)? What is the height of the contour running through the word 'Mill' (791 621)? What is different about this contour from most of the other contours, and why do you think it is drawn in this way?

(iii) If you cannot find a number on the contour, you may have to count in 25-foot jumps upwards or downwards from a contour that *is* numbered. What is the height of the highest contour shown at 776 629? It will help you if you look northwards to a lower contour that is numbered.

(iv) The height above sea level of Saint Mary's Church (785 626) is obviously 100 feet, for the contour line runs right through it. Estimate the height above sea level of the house called the 'Meads', just to the north-west of the church. As it lies roughly between the 100-foot contour and the 125-foot contour, how high above sea level is it? Estimate the heights above sea level, or elevations, of the building at 793 622 and New Barn at 780 629.

▼ Figure 3.9   Vertical view of Dartington, with the sea at its present level

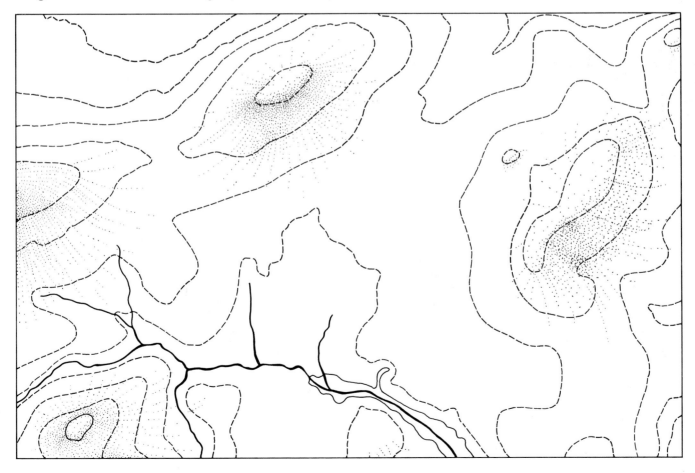

Activity 3:13

(a) Compare Map 3 and the side view of Dartington shown in Figure 3.8. Find Yarner Beacon (778 620) and the sloping ground between Broom Park Estate (783 624) and Lownard (783 623). Describe the slopes in both places. Are they steep or gentle?

(b) Now say what you notice about the spacing of the contours on these two hillsides. Which is closely spaced and which is widely spaced?

(c) Generally, we can say that: *where there are no contours the map shows flat land*, or no slope; *widely spaced contours show gentle slopes*; and *closely spaced contours show steep slopes*. Find, and give six-figure grid references for, two examples of each kind of slope on the map. If possible, check the steepness of each by looking at Figure 3.8.

(d) (i) If you walked towards Dartington Hall along the road beside High Cross Hill House (793 624), would you be going up or down a slope? (ii) Similarly, if you walked towards Huxham's Cross, along the A384 past The Parsonage (783 628), would you be walking up or down a slope?

Activity 3:14

Note that the contour numbers tell us which direction on the slope is uphill. The numbers stand upslope. Look at the contour numbers in North Wood on Map 3. This slope, which faces south-east, is said to have a south-east ASPECT. Aspect is the direction a slope faces. Find, and give six-figure grid references to, slopes that have north, east, south and west aspects.

Smaller and smaller

What do a doll's house, a train set, a plastic aeroplane made from a kit and a miniature tea service have in common? They are all toys, yes but they are also smaller versions of the real-sized objects.

In much the same way, the objects in maps are drawn smaller than they actually are. Look at Lownard Cottage as it appears on Figure 1.6, Map 1 and Map 3. It is like taking a helicopter ride: as you rise up in the air, the house looks smaller and smaller. If you rose much higher, what would happen to your view of the cottage?

We will now try to answer how and why maps do this to the landscape. Let us turn back to your classroom to help you find the answers.

Activity 3:15

(a) Look at Figure 3.10, which is a pencil sharpener drawn to its correct size, as seen from above. Choose an object, such as an eraser or pencil box, which is smaller than the page in your writing book or file. Carefully measure around the edge of the object and draw it to its correct size on your paper, again as seen from above. Give it a title, label the measurements and underneath it write '1 centimetre on the page represents 1 centimetre on the object'.

(b) What problems would you have if you tried to draw this book, *A First Course in Mapwork*, on your paper? One way round the problem is to measure its sides and divide these measurements by two. Draw the book on your paper, using these new measurements. Give your drawing a title, label it with the measurements of its true size, and write underneath it '1 centimetre on the page represents 2 centimetres on the object.'

(c) Now measure the top of your desk or table. It is so large that even dividing its true size by two will not make it small enough to fit on your page. This time, make 1 centimetre on the page represent 10 centimetres on the object. Draw it to these reduced measurements on your paper.

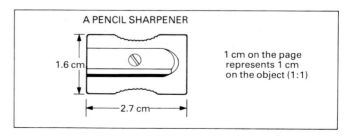

▲ Figure 3.10   A pencil sharpener drawn to true scale

Measure the other objects on your desk and draw them to the same scale on the desk plan in your book. Put them in their correct places. Give the plan you have drawn a title, label the true measurements, and write an appropriate scale statement beneath it.

What you have been doing is drawing objects to SCALE. This means you have been drawing things in sizes proportional to the actual ones. It should be obvious that to get a map of anything as large as a house, school or town onto a piece of paper, you either need the help of a magician or the use of a scale!

Choosing the right scale was not obvious to the characters in Lewis Carroll's *Sylvie and Bruno Concluded*:

'What do you consider the *largest* map that would be really useful?'
'About six inches to the mile.'
'Only *six inches*!' exclaimed Mein Herr. 'We very soon got to six *yards* to the mile. Then we tried a *hundred* yards to the mile. And then came the grandest idea of all! We actually made a map of the country on the scale of *a mile to the mile*!'
''Have you used it much?' I enquired.
'It has never been spread out, yet,' said Mein Herr: 'the farmers objected; they said it would cover the whole country and shut out the sunlight! So we now use the country itself, as its own map, and I assure you it does nearly as well.'

As you can see, choosing the right scale is really a matter of choosing the most convenient one.

Activity 3:16

(a) Draw a map of your classroom to a convenient scale. First measure the room, and then discuss with your neighbours what that convenient scale might be before you start to draw.

(b) (i) The scale of the map in Figure 1.6, pages 8–9, can be written down in several ways. If you have your own copy of that map, write on it the following information about its scale:

1 centimetre to 2 metres (called a Statement Scale)
1:200 (Statement Scale)
1 to 200 (Statement Scale)
$\frac{1}{200}$ (Representive Fraction)
0 2 4 (Linear Scale)

These all mean that 1 centimetre on the map represents 200 centimetres on the ground (another Statement Scale).
(ii) Draw your classroom to this scale.
(iii) If you were to draw your classroom to the scale of Map 1, which is 1 to 2500, what problems might you find?

Plan a trail

The countryside around this area is very inviting, so it attracts lots of tourists. Usually they park in a newly made car park in the field at 787 622 (see Map 2). It is next to a craft shop in what used to be Shinner's Bridge Farm. The next activity expects you to use most of the skills you have learned in this chapter and Chapter 2.

Activity 3:17

To give the tourists a chance to see more places of interest in Dartington, plan a trail, linking features of the landscape. You may choose to plan either a Historical, Farm, or Wildlife Trail.

(a) The starting point is marked on Map 3. Places of interest are marked on the map, and details about each are listed in Figure 3.11.

(b) Mark on tracing paper your chosen features and try to plan a walk that takes in at least six points of interest.

(c) All of the area is open to you, but you must plan walks around the edges of the fields. Stiles can be built if needed. Look at the key, Key 2A, and note the symbols for footpaths, tracks and roads.

(d) Try to keep distances short and avoid steep slopes. Remember what you would feel like if you were doing the walk.

● HISTORICAL TRAIL

1 The three-metre high Deer Park stone wall here surrounds a medieval park where noblemen from Dartington Hall used to hunt deer.
2 Staverton Bridge, built in AD1410, is a fine example of a pack horse bridge.

3 The ford at Stillpool was a busy crossing place in the distant past when tin, hides and wool were brought down from Dartmoor on the way to the old seaport of Totnes.
4 The earthworks in North Wood are the remains of an Iron Age camp. Archaeologists have found the remains of Roman pottery here.
5 The line of trees marks another ancient trackway following the ridge top, where a Celtic Cross once stood.
6 Dartington Hall, built by John Holand, dates from the fourteenth century. It is the largest and most important medieval house in the West of England. In its grounds stands a tower; all that remains of the old St. Mary's Church.
7 After a large part of the old St. Mary's Church was pulled down in 1878, a new church was built on this site in 1880. It was of similar design and contained much of the material from the former building.
8 The village of Week is one of the oldest in this area. Its thatched-roofed and stone-walled buildings have changed little over the centuries.

▲ FARM TRAIL

1 Old Parsonage Farm specialises in dairy farming. These farm buildings were built in 1931, to a design which was advanced for the times.
2 This ruined set of farm buildings was burnt down in 1968. They were outlying barns for the Shinners Bridge Farm and were used as a grain store and possibly for grinding cereals too.
3 A hedgerow calculated to be approximately six hundred years old. Many hedges have been removed in Devon because they are expensive to maintain and larger fields are easier to work with modern machinery.
4 Here a section through the huge hedgerow bank shows its core of earth and stone. It forms an important wildlife habitat.
5 The fields to the west are called Higher and Lower Newground, so-called because they were reclaimed from woodland. The heavy clay in this field means that it is best kept as permanent grass.
6 Alongside this concrete road, to the east, is Sneezles Prairie named after the first farm manager. In the 1930s he removed the hedges from twelve fields to make this big, twenty-eight hectare field.
7 The soil here has naturally moved downhill and is much deeper than at the top of the slope. The collection of soil on horse-drawn sledges was widely practised on these steep Devon slopes and was certainly carried out last in Dartington in 1938.
8 These fields are used for growing cereals and root crops which are used as cattle feed in winter when the grass stops growing.

■ WILDLIFE TRAIL

1 In North Wood there is a stand of Californian Redwoods that is the fastest growing stand of coniferous trees in Europe. Look for goldcrests, wood pigeons and ravens.
2 At Stillpool the River Dart contains trout and salmon. A flash of blue reveals the Kingfisher, fishing alongside the neighbouring herons.
3 This field is steep so it has not been ploughed or sprayed with herbicide. Wild grasses abound here, encouraging butterflies like the Meadow Brown, Speckled Wood and Small Copper.
4 In this damp patch, water-loving plants such as flag iris grow and dragonflies can be seen.
5 This mixed wood containing oak, beech, sycamore and wild cherry lets in more light than coniferous trees, encouraging a generous growth of bluebells, primroses and wild garlic.

6 The Bidwell Brook is a lively stream cutting through a beautiful limestone valley. Look here for mallard ducks, dippers and, if you are lucky, water voles.
7 The limestone in this quarry contains fossils that are millions of years old. Growing on it are mosses, ferns and lichens.
8 Buckham Park Barn is a perfect habitat for bats and barn owls.

▲ Figure 3.11 Places of interest in Dartington

(e) Produce a written guide, stating the following details:
(i) Six-figure grid reference of each point.
(ii) Distance from each point to the next point. Remember to use the scale on Key 2A or the map border.
(iii) Whether the next section of the trail is uphill or downhill.
(iv) The approximate compass direction of the next section.

(f) Lastly, draw a simple sketch map to be used as the guideboard at the start of the trail. Mark only the main features of the walk. Use your own symbols, give it a key and a title and draw it at a scale of roughly 1:5000. This means it will be about twice the size of Map 3, the O.S. 1:10 560 map.

CHAPTER 4

Totnes and District

What can you learn from this chapter?

It can:

1 Show you some of the wide variety of maps and their uses
2 Introduce you to the O.S. 1:25 000 Pathfinder Map
3 Let you practise skills to do with location, distance, direction, symbol, height and scale
4 Help you learn some new map skills
5 Show you how to play a game using map skills

Images of Totnes

Just three kilometres from Dartington lies the historic town of Totnes. The poster shown in Figure 4.1 presents an almost fairytale image of the town. The artist has exaggerated sizes, stretched roofs and created impossible roadways.

Activity 4:1

(a) (i) What impression do you think the artist was trying to give of the town of Totnes?
(ii) Explain what you think might be the main purpose of the picture.

(b) (i) Say which features of the townscape could never have been seen together at the same time.
(ii) What things might the artist have deliberately left out of his image of Totnes? Try to explain why he did this.

This curious picture of the real world is very similar to the often distorted MENTAL MAPS we all carry around in our heads. In a geography project completed by a school student, over fifty people were interviewed and asked to draw a sketch map of Totnes. These look something like

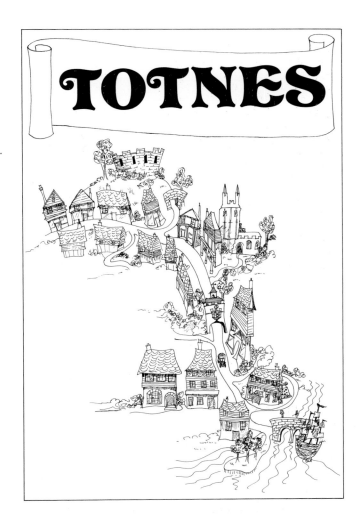

▲ Figure 4.1 An artist's view of Totnes

43

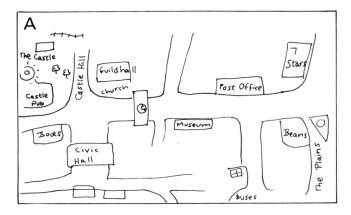

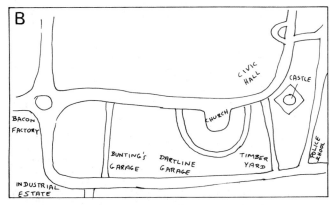

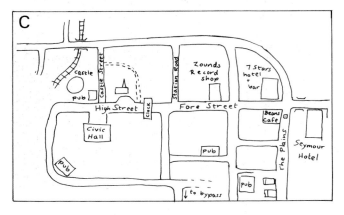

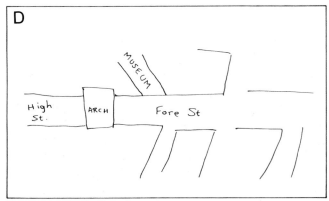

▲ Figure 4.2   Mental maps of Totnes

the maps in our minds. Four of these maps are shown in Figure 4.2. Short pen-pictures of six people who were interviewed are given below.

Simon Birchall (age 32) is a policeman who has lived and worked in Totnes for the last five years.

Chris Braithwaite (24) is a lorry driver for a scrap metal dealer in Buckfastleigh, a few miles away. He regularly drives from there to Torbay, using Coronation Road, which bypasses the town centre. On the interview day he had stopped to buy cigarettes.

Ernie Oliver (19) has lived all his life in Totnes. He works in Ashburton as a labourer, but claims to be more interested in going out with his mates.

Margaret Lowson (65) has lived on the Plains, near the river, for the last 40 years, with her husband. Arthritis means she cannot get around so well these days.

Mandy Wilson (52) is a tourist from Leeds. She is staying in Torbay and has spent 20 minutes in the town since arriving by coach on the Plains.

Joe Howarth (38) is also a tourist, but he is from London. He has been staying at the Seven Stars Hotel for the last week, with his wife and 13-year-old son and 10-year-old daughter.

Activity 4:2

(a) Among the six people featured in the pen-pictures are the four people who drew the maps. Decide which person drew each map, and give reasons for your choice. Note that the Figure 4.2(B) is drawn from a different viewpoint than the others.

(b) For the remaining two people, suggest how complete their maps might be and the kind of features they might have drawn on them.

(c) Using information from the mental maps, try to name some of the landmarks on Figure 4.1.

(d) (i) Mental maps are fun to collect and analyse. Your class should agree upon a small local study area and, as a first step, each of you draw your own map of that area. Be sure to include all the features that you think are important. To extend the study, give family, friends and neighbours a pencil and paper and the same instructions. Note who drew each map and, if possible, record other details about the people that you think are relevant.

▲ Figure 4.3   An aerial photograph of Totnes, Devon

(ii) To analyse the maps, pin them on the wall and compare them with an accurate map of the study area. Count how many features are included in each mental map. Note which parts of the area seem to be best known and which are least known. Look out for distortions such as the straightening of winding roads, or features in the wrong places.
(iii) Now try to explain each map in terms of the person who drew it. Answer such questions as: Where does the person live, work, or play most of the time? How long have they lived there? How well do they get around and what form of transport do they use? Their age might be important too. Think of anything else that might explain why they drew their maps in a particular way.
(iv) Lastly, try to assemble your drawings into one map that presents a summary of the mental maps of the study area. Count how often each feature is included on all the maps. Then draw a summary map by marking, with a dark colour, those features included frequently and use lighter and lighter colours for the features that are included less frequently.

(e) Remember that the mental maps people draw reflect the image they have of an area. Not everyone is good at drawing, so it may not be a very accurate copy of what is in their heads. But a study of mental maps raises important issues.
(i) How important is your own mental map of the world, or parts of the world, to you?
(ii) In what ways are the mental maps that are inside our heads useful?
(iii) What are the problems and dangers of faulty or poor mental maps?
(iv) How can your mental map be improved?

A different, more recognisable, image of Totnes is given by the aerial photograph shown in Figure 4.3. It shows part of the town centre, including the High Street and Castle.

Activity 4:3

(a) Which of the landmarks illustrated by Figure 4.1 can you find in the photograph?

(b) Was the photograph taken in the same direction as Figure 4.1?

(c) Working in pairs, place a piece of tracing paper over the photograph and mark on it as many features as you can identify from the mental maps shown in Figure 4.2.

The Ordnance Survey also produces its own images of Totnes. Map 4 is a 1:2500 map of some of Totnes town centre. (Note that it is the same scale as Map 1 on pages 18–19.)

Activity 4:4

(a) Compare Map 4 with Map 1 in Chapter 2. In a sentence or two, describe the main differences between the landscapes they show.

(b) (i) If you can, share two books and orient the map, Map 4, and the photograph, Figure 4.3.
(ii) What is the reason for doing this?
(iii) In what direction was the camera facing?

(c) Add to your tracing, started in Activity 4:3, South Street, The Grove, Victoria Street, Coronation Road, Fore Street, High Street and the Plains.

(d) If you were exploring the town for the first time, which places would you visit first of all and why?

Much of Totnes is very old and the map holds a surprising amount of information about the historic town, if you know where to look. The next activity will allow you to build a historical image of the townscape.

Activity 4:5

Read the following historical account, identifying on Map 4 the places printed in italic.

Before AD 450: *Fore Street and High Street* have been an important routeway for over 2000 years. Other ancient trackways are also preserved in the street plan, one by the line of *Castle Street* and another southwards along the *Plains*.

▲ Figure 4.4   Fore Street and East Gate, Totnes

▲ Figure 4.5   The Castle and North Gate, Totnes

Map 4

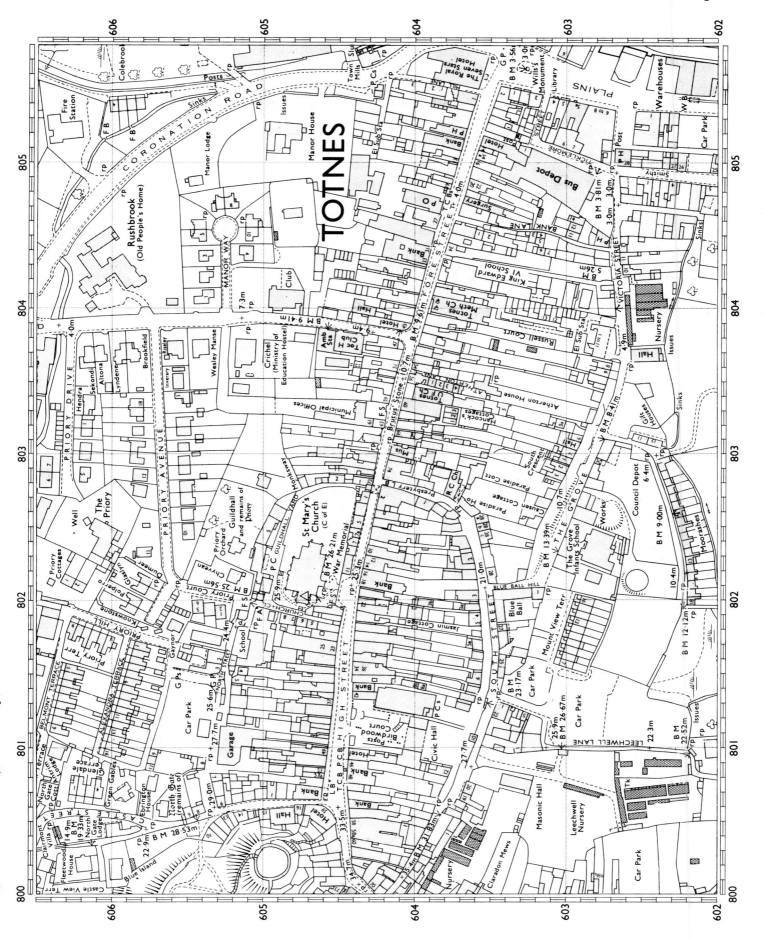

TOTNES

AD 450–1066: Attacking Danes, in the tenth century, forced the Saxons to build a fortified settlement on top of the hill. It had an oval pattern, seen today by the line of *South Street*, *Guildhall Yard* and *North Street*. It probably took the form of a wooden stockade with gates at the three main openings. *East Gate* (which is the arch seen in the modern view in Figure 4.4) and *North Gate* (which is the arched bridge seen in the modern view in Figure 4.5) can both be found on the map. In the Domesday Book of 1086, the stockade enclosed most of the 100 or so recorded houses. Just outside East Gate, several other houses were protected by an additional earthbank and stockade along the line of *The Grove*, *Victoria Street*, and *Ticklemore Street*.

AD 1066–1200: The Normans built the present *castle* (see Figure 4.5) and its *ditches*, a priory and a small church. Each house owned the land from the main street to the stockade. This formed long, narrow strips, commonly used in the way shown in Figure 4.6.

AD 1500–1900: Some changes took place in the 16th to 19th centuries. *St. Mary's Church* was built with profits from the export of cloth, leather and tin from nearby Dartmoor. The priory was knocked down and the *Guildhall* (seen in Figure 4.7) was built on its foundations. Trading was important and the *Town Mills* were built for grinding corn. The town's prosperity increased then decreased during this last period. By the 19th century, the town was a quiet, rural place. The bridge was rebuilt in 1826. *Station Road* was constructed. It joins Fore Street just to the east of the Brutus Stone.

AD 1900 onwards: In the present century, a bypass, called *Coronation Road*, was constructed to avoid the narrow, congested main street. A fire in 1955 made way for a new *Civic Hall* off the south side of the High Street. Today, Totnes is a bustling, thriving tourist and market town.

Activity 4:6

(a) Use tracing paper to make a map of the historical growth of Totnes. Trace the features from the map that are in italics in the historical account. Use a different colour for the set of features in each paragraph. Add a key, title, north point and scale to your tracing.

(b) Study the house plot shown in Figure 4.6 and those on Figure 4.3. Give the addresses of three houses where this courtyard plan is well-preserved.

(c) Using map evidence, give three present-day uses of the strips of land behind the main houses. How else might modern shopkeepers use this land?

(d) Each of the grid squares on the map represents an area of one hectare (100 square metres, or about the size of two soccer pitches). Approximately how large was the old Saxon town inside the original oval fortified settlement?

▲ Figure 4.6   Totnes house plot in Norman times

▲ Figure 4.7   The Guildhall, Totnes

48

(e) Draw a picture of the Saxon town of Totnes as you think it might have looked when it was being attacked by Danes.

(f) Imagine that you are the producer of a television programme to be made about the history and buildings of Totnes. Write part of a producer's script, with directions and comments to the camera crew, using the prints shown in Figures 4.4, 4.5, and 4.7 as three of your shots. You need to specify where the camera is to be placed, the direction to face, whether the camera should focus and zoom in on a feature or pan round to show a general view.

(g) Explain how historical maps, like the one you drew in Activity 4:6(a), may be of use.

The world is full of map-like images, like those of Totnes. In fact, you will meet hundreds and hundreds of them in your life. They may not always be as detailed or as accurately drawn as an Ordnance Survey map, but recognising them and understanding why they were made and how they are used is very important in everyday life. Apart from the maps we carry, sometimes unknowingly, in our minds, just think of others you have seen and maybe used. Collecting, studying, and understanding them can be very interesting.

Activity 4:7

Make a collection of all the maps you can find over the next few days. Look for them in books, newspapers, magazines, advertisements, in the street, in shops, public buildings and indeed everywhere. For those that you can cut out and carry, answer the following questions:

(a) (i) Who? Find out which person or organisation was responsible for making the map.
(ii) Why? Write a sentence to summarise the main reasons for making the map.
(iii) When? Try to find out when it was made.
(iv) Where? Name the area shown on the map.
(v) What? Describe the main features that the map-maker thought were important enough to include and, if possible, try to suggest features that were not included.
(vi) How? Describe the way in which the map was drawn. For example, has the map a bird's eye

viewpoint, a grid system for locating things, a scale, a northpoint and so on? Pay attention to the range and nature of symbols used.

(b) Rank your maps in order of preference. Put those that you like the most at the top of your list and those you like the least at the foot of the list. give reasons for your choices.

Among your collection, do you have any imaginary maps? Inventing maps purely from imagination can be fun. J.R.R. Tolkien invented the Middle Earth in his book *The Lord of the Rings*. C.S. Lewis created Narnia. Sometimes writers base their imaginary world on part of the real world, like the maps by Arthur Ransome in his books about the Swallows and the Amazons. Do you know any of these maps? Think of other books that include imaginary maps.

Activity 4:8

Try drawing your own imaginary map. Choose one of the following places:

(a) Part of a newly explored planet.

(b) The lost continent of Atlantis.

(c) A pirate's island.

(d) A city of the year AD 3000.
Use your own symbols and make up your own place names. Remember to give your map a title, northpoint, key and scale.

The Pathfinder Map

Map 5 (page 55) is the Ordnance Survey's PATHFINDER MAP of Totnes and part of its district. What do you think a Pathfinder Map's main uses might be? What landscape changes may have happened in this popular holiday and retirement area since the map was drawn? What immediate differences do you notice between this map and the 1:10 560 map, Map 3?

One of the major differences between them is the addition of more colour to the 1:25 000 Pathfinder Map. In Chapter 2 you learned how to use a key to understand many symbols. The key to Map 5 is Key 3 on page 36.

```
        ~~~~~ ,

You've got a ------- mind.
You're on the road to ⊠.
You might just as well ⸙ ⸙
your --------etic attempts to
take my place or you may end
up in the ═══A 31 (T)═══ of the
nearest ⫘ car! It's no
good ══✕══ with Max w
We know you've been ⤙
away the money you stole
under ⤙ and key ever since
you ◄┅┅┅► ed your way out
of the Twr , but you're
◄┅┅► it a bit fine if you
think you're going to
have enough money to get
you out of the country
before the Spr.
So let me just warn you,
before you try to ⸌⸍ off
with the money, make sure
I get my cut, or they'll
be ⸌⸍ ⸌⸍ ing about your
mysterious disappearance.
```

▲ Figure 4.8   Coded message

Activity 4:9

(a) List the colours used on a 1:25 000 map.

(b) Which colours seem most appropriate to the features they represent and why? Which seem less appropriate and why? What reason might the map-makers have for using colours which seem inappropriate?

(c) Compare the key for the 1:25 000 map, Key 3, and the key for the 1:2500 map, Key 1. Name two symbols that have been left off the 1:25 000 map and two extra ones that have been added.

(d) Another difference is that some symbols are changed in appearance. Explain the different presentation of road symbols on the 1:25 000 and 1:2500 maps.

(e) Some of the 1:25 000 map symbols look like the objects they represent, while others do not. Give four examples of this, naming two which do and two which do not.

Activity 4:10

(a) In Chapter 2, the symbols were likened to a language. To understand a language it is often necessary to use a dictionary, which in this case is the map key. Use Key 3 to decode the letter shown in Figure 4.8, sent in code by one dangerous criminal to another.

(b) Try your hand at writing a letter to your friend in this symbol code, or you could write a reply to the letter in Figure 4.8, or a party invitation.

Activity 4:11

(a) Draw a grid square to the correct size for a 1:25 000 map and draw on it symbols, at the same scale, to illustrate the following description.

The land slopes evenly from the north from around 500 metres to 200 metres. A trunk road, running east to west across the centre, is crossed by a multiple-track railway that runs north-east to south-west. Just to the west of the level crossing, where the road and railway cross, is a railway station. A small village with a Post Office, School and a Church with a spire, is located around the level crossing. Most of the north-west corner of the grid square is covered by coniferous trees. The extreme south-east corner is marshy.

(b) In another empty grid square, draw your own landscape using the 1:25 000 map symbols, and write a description of it. Exchange just the descriptions with your neighbours, keeping your own sketch map. See if you can both draw accurate maps from the descriptions.

(c) From a verbal description of a grid square on Map 5, given to you by your teacher, identify the square on the map.

(d) Study grid square 79 61 on Map 5 and choose a place for a picnic. Give a six-figure grid reference to the point and give reasons for your choice.

In Chapter 3 you learned that the scale of a map is the way the size of an object compares with its real size on the ground. One way of looking at this is to compare Figure 1.6 and all the O.S. maps you have seen so far in this book (Maps 1, 3, 4 and 5).

Activity 4:12

Place a piece of tracing paper over Map 5 and use a ruler and pencil to draw rectangles to show the area covered by Figure 1.6 and each of the O.S. maps in Chapters 2, 3, and 4. Label each rectangle with its scale.

Activity 4:13

(a) A quick way of making sense of scales like 1:25 000 is to say:

One centimetre on the map represents 25 000 centimetres or 250 metres on the ground. You need only knock off two noughts, i.e. 25 0ØØ, to find out the distance in metres. The same method can be used with other scales. Copy Figure 4.9 and write in the missing sentences.

(b) As you move from 1:10 000 to 1:200, the maps are becoming larger in scale. As you move from 1:25 000 to 1:250 000, the maps are becoming smaller in scale. Going back to Activity 4.12, look at your tracings and write a general statement linking the scales of the maps with the amount of ground area they cover.

Becoming larger in scale	On a 1:200 map, 1 centimetre is the same as 2 metres on the ground.
	On a 1:2500, ...
	On a 1:10 000, ...
	On a 1:25 000 map, ...
	On a 1:50 000, ...
Becoming smaller in scale	On a 1:250 000, ...

▲ Figure 4.9   Scales and quick conversions

The road system, shown in Map 5, has grown over thousands of years. Nowadays, the main roads spread out from Totnes like the spokes of a wheel. Remember in Chapter 2 you found out about eight points of the compass. In roughly what directions do the roads go?

The eight-point compass rose can be further subdivided to make a total of sixteen points. This means you can be more accurate when judging direction. The extra eight points on Figure 4.10 have been numbered and three of them have been named.

Activity 4:14

(a) Copy Figure 4.10 and name the remaining points. Note that number 1 is a direction a little to the north of north-east, hence its label, north-north-east. Notice that number two is a direction east of north-east, hence east-north-east.

(b) Use Map 5 and Figure 4.10 and write down the compass directions:
(i) from Totnes Castle (800 605) to Littlehempston church (812 626);
(ii) from Totnes Castle to North Wood (787 635);

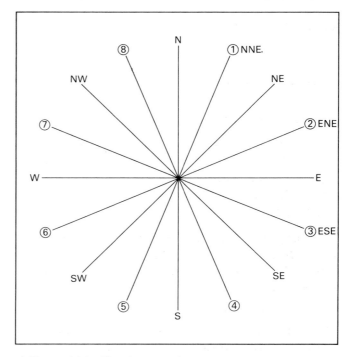

▲ Figure 4.10   The sixteen point compass rose

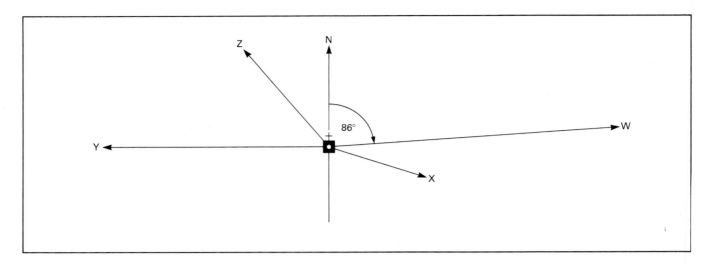

▲ Figure 4.11   Bearings from St Mary's Church, Totnes

(iii) from Berry Pomeroy church (829 610) to Totnes Castle;
(iv) from Littlehempston church to Netherton (825 624).

(c) A different way of learning the sixteen compass points can be done in your classroom if its layout is suitable. Seat sixteen people in a circle, facing inwards towards one person in the middle. The one in the middle points at a person in the circle, who becomes north. After counting ten seconds, the one in the middle points at four more people, one after the other. They must immediately call out their compass directions, relating to the person who is north. If they fail to do so correctly, they must leave the compass and let another person from outside the circle take their place. The game continues with the person in the middle selecting a new north point each time. The counting can be lengthened or shortened, depending on how good you are! The aim is to remain seated in the circle as long as possible.

A pilot flying over the Atlantic needs to have a more accurate direction than something like 'a little bit south of west-south-west.' He could end up many kilometres away from the airport he wants to find. Even hikers, caught in a mountain fog, need precise directions to find their way. There is a long-established system that does just this. You may have met it already in your mathematics lesson if you have learned that a full circle has 360 degrees.

The compass can be shown as a circle, divided by 360 lines, or degrees, instead of just

16. Each line represents a particular direction and they are numbered from 0 to 360. Study a 180° protractor, which can be used to demonstrate half of the circle. The lines on it, when used in compass work, are called BEARINGS. Bearings are, therefore, directions measured in degrees from north. A protractor can also be used to measure these bearings.

Activity 4:15

(a) Place a protractor over Figure 4.11 to check the bearing, in degrees, from St. Mary's Church, Totnes, to point W. Place it with the 0 to 180 degree line along the north line, centred at St. Mary's Church. Point W should read 86 degrees. Now measure the bearings from St. Mary's Church to points X, Y, and Z. Note that bearings are always measured in degrees from north, in a clockwise direction.

Place the protractor over St. Mary's Church (802 604) on Map 5, using the grid lines to help you position its 0°/180° base line in a north-south direction. Find out what features of the landscape can be found at W, X, Y and Z. If the only protractor you have is marked from 0° to 180° then think of the method you must use to find Y and Z.

(b) In Activity 2:8 in Chapter 2, you solved a small problem that often faces the local electricity board. The planning department of that board, however, frequently solves larger problems, too. Consider the following problem:

There are proposals to enlarge the village of Littlehempston. Building will take place in the fields around 810 627. This means extra strain on the electricity supply, which is sufficient only for existing needs. To increase the electricity supply, new overhead cables must be built. The only supply source for this situation is the Dun Cross transformer located at 776 618. There are two possible connections. The first is a line running north of Cott, the second, a line running south of Cott. You are not allowed to build overhead cables over housing. The cost of overhead cable construction is £10 000 per kilometre.

(i) Plan both routes carefully, marking them on a tracing. Note how direct the power lines are that already appear on the map.

(ii) Now write a report comparing the alternatives, including a careful description of each route, stating the bearings in degrees of each straight section from Dun Cross to Littlehempston. Work out the distance and approximate cost of each route and include it in the report. On the basis of this report, suggest which route you recommend.

(iii) Suggest which groups of people in this area might object to these plans and explain what you think their arguments might be.

(iv) Plan one alternative route that would lessen the visual impact of the power lines on this attractive countryside. The lessening in environmental damage may well be worth the extra cost of a longer route. Remember, buried power lines are very expensive indeed.

Chapter 3 introduced you to the idea of a contour. One contour tells us about height, while several together tell us about slope. But, if you hold Map 5 away from you, the contours make confusing patterns. In places they look like thumbprints, but mostly they seem to wiggle aimlessly across the map. With a little practice you can learn how to recognise the shape of individual landforms. Each one makes a distinctive pattern, much like a set of fingerprints. Study the landform sketches in Figure 4.12 and the contour patterns they make. Then do Activity 4.16 on page 59.

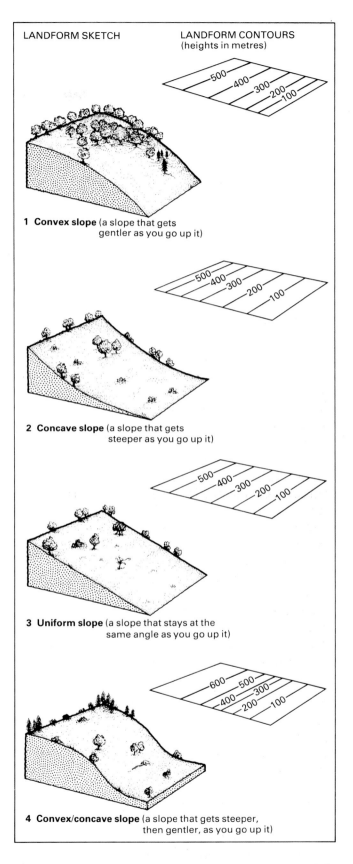

LANDFORM SKETCH   LANDFORM CONTOURS
                        (heights in metres)

1 Convex slope (a slope that gets gentler as you go up it)

2 Concave slope (a slope that gets steeper as you go up it)

3 Uniform slope (a slope that stays at the same angle as you go up it)

4 Convex/concave slope (a slope that gets steeper, then gentler, as you go up it)

▲ Figure 4.12   Contour fingerprints (continued on page 54)

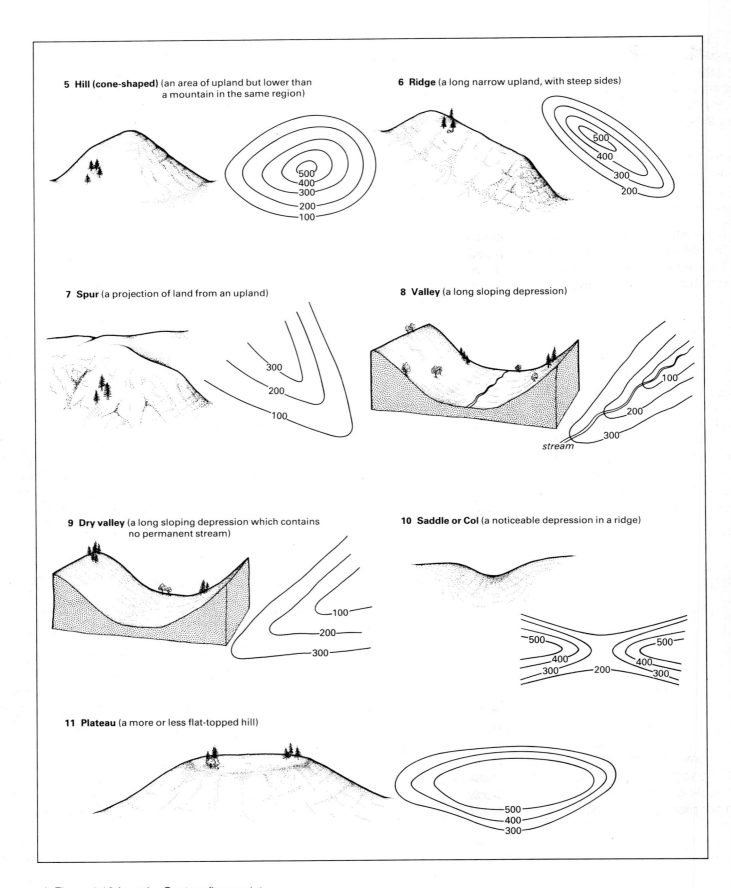

5 Hill (cone-shaped) (an area of upland but lower than
a mountain in the same region)

6 Ridge (a long narrow upland, with steep sides)

7 Spur (a projection of land from an upland)

8 Valley (a long sloping depression)

9 Dry valley (a long sloping depression which contains
no permanent stream)

10 Saddle or Col (a noticeable depression in a ridge)

11 Plateau (a more or less flat-topped hill)

▲ Figure 4.12 (cont.)   Contour fingerprints

Map 5

Map 5 Totnes (1:25 000)

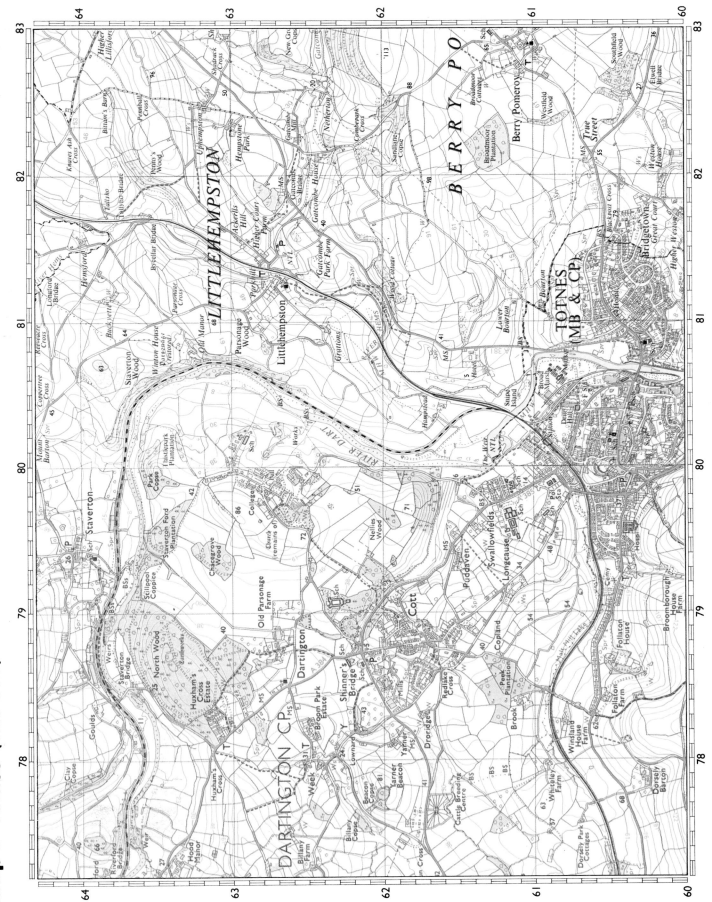

BERRY PO

TOTNES (MB & CP)

Bridgetown

LITTLEHEMPSTON

DARTINGTON CP

Map 6 Swansea Bay (1:50 000)

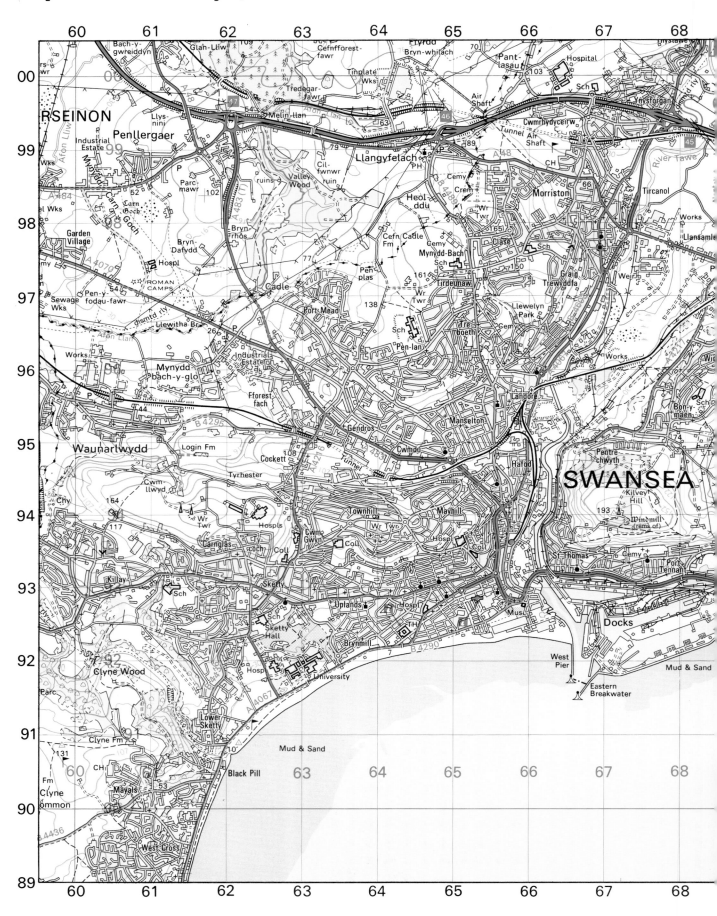

Map 6

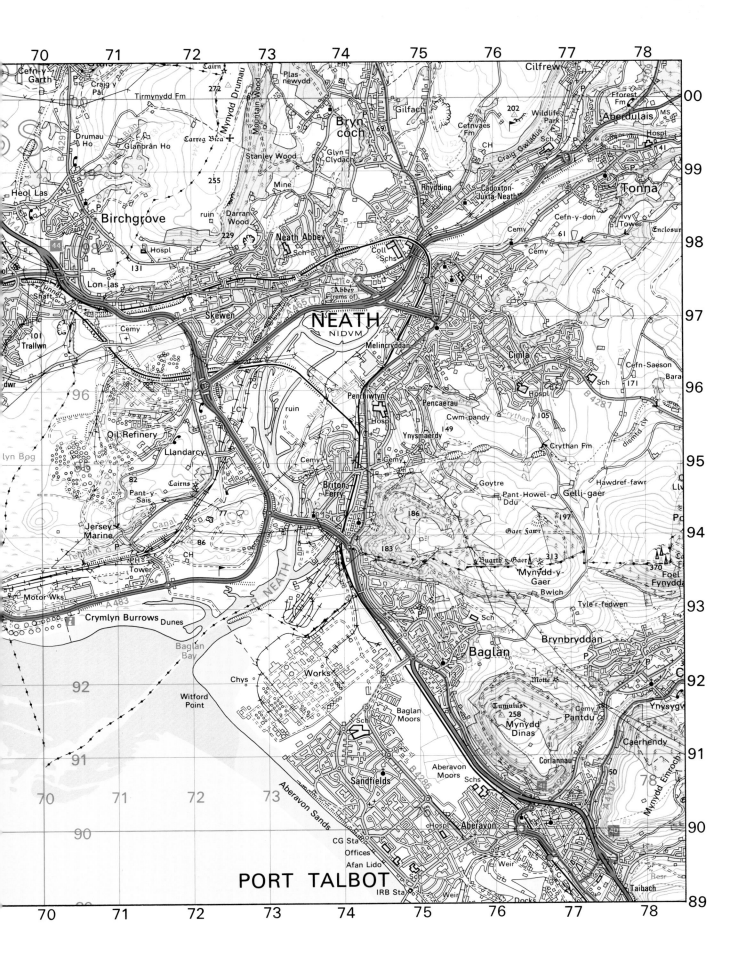

Map 7 Rickmansworth (1:50 000)

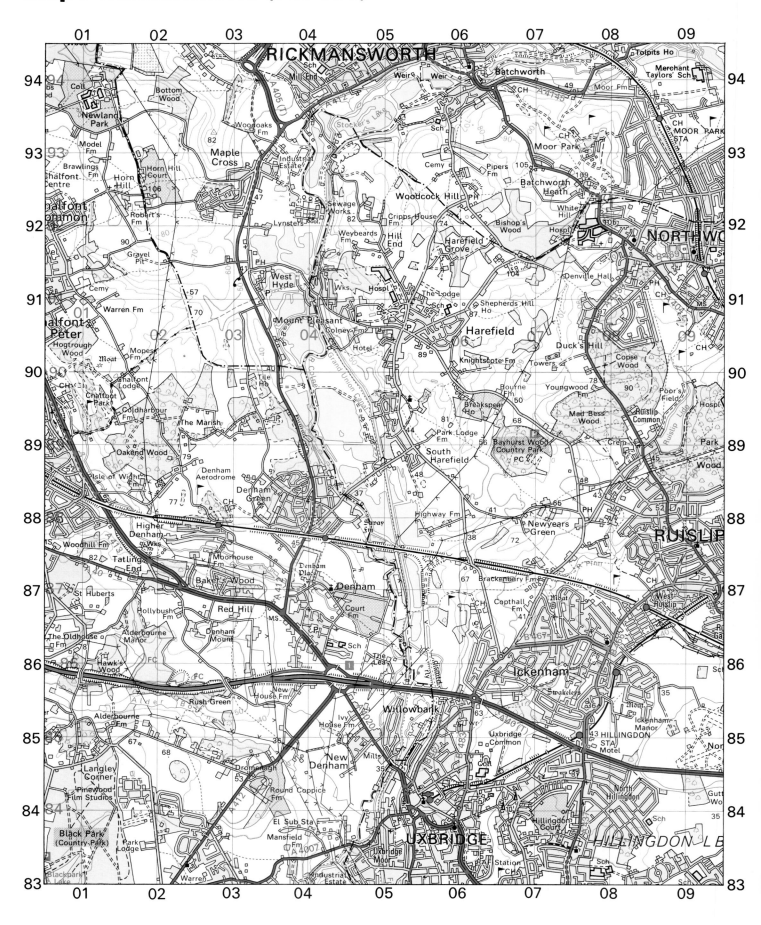

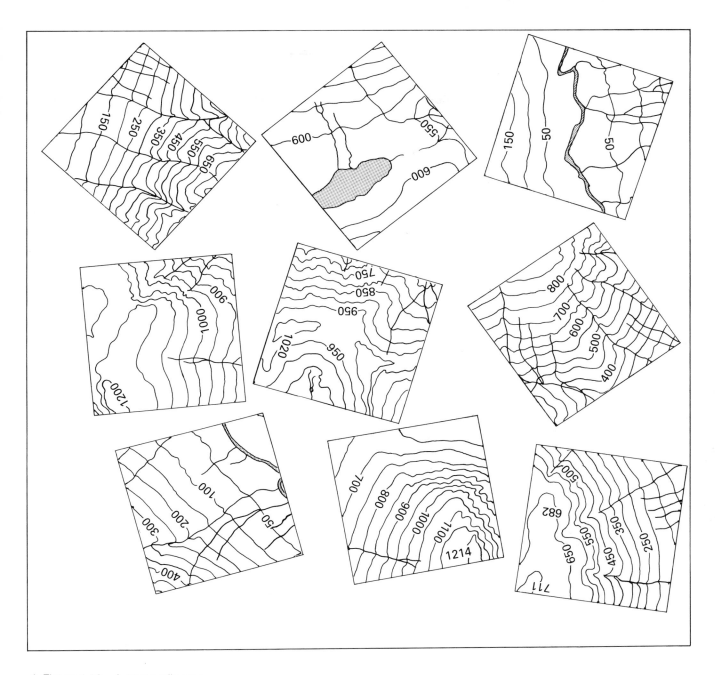

▲ Figure 4.13   A contour jigsaw

Activity 4:16

(a) Use the set of contour fingerprints in Figure 4.12 to find an example of each landform on Map 3. Give a grid square reference to each and remember that the shapes will not necessarily match exactly.

(b) (i) Use copies of Figure 4.13. Cut out the nine grid squares and try to fit together the contour jigsaw, sticking them down on a backing sheet of paper or card. Remember to look carefully at the shapes and heights of the contours to help you.
(ii) On the completed jigsaw, use the following labels to name the features of this mountainous landscape: flat land; concave slope; cliff-like slope; ridge with both steep and gentle sides; gulley; steep-sided valley; mountain top; convex slope.

Totnes Car Rally

Teams in the Monte Carlo Rally have to be expert map readers. Even local rallying demands an ability to read maps quickly and well. The aim of this skilful game is to race round the course as quickly as you can, trying to gain as many bonus points and as few penalty points as possible. To be successful, you will need to use many of the ideas and skills you have learned in the first four chapters of this book.

Activity 4:17

(a) The rules are as follows:
(i) Your teacher is the rally controller and race judge and you may race by yourself, although it is probably better to drive in teams of two.
(ii) The object is to choose the correct route from place to place on Map 5 (page 55), in the shortest possible time. The route for each stage will be given to you by your teacher on completion of the previous stage.

```
TOTNES CAR RALLY TIME SHEET

NAME(s) OF DRIVER(s) _____
STAGE ONE
Starting Place _____
Destination _____
Starting time _____
Arrival time _____
Time allowed _____
Time taken _____
Observation problems 1 _____
                     2 _____
                     3 _____
Points at start of stage _____
Observation Bonus Points _____
Time Bonus Points _____
Sub total _____
Time Penalty Points _____
Route Penalty Points _____
Sub total _____

Total points at end of stage _____
```

▲ Figure 4.14   Totnes car rally time sheet

(iii) You start with 100 points to which you add Time Bonus Points if you finish inside the time limit set by the race controller. If you finish outside the time limit, Time Penalty Points count against you. One minute equals one point in both cases.
(iv) On each rally stage, Observation Bonus Points are available if you can solve the observation problems. The number of such bonus points available varies with the difficulty of the problem. Collecting Observation Points is optional.
(v) The best rally drivers choose the exact correct route. Route Penalty Points are deducted for missing the correct route. These are deducted at the discretion of the race controller, but are roughly one point for a minor miss to 10 points for a route that is completely wrong.
(vi) Make out a Totnes Car Rally Time Sheet to record your points, for four stages, like the example in Figure 4.14. You need to trace your route onto tracing paper as you go, with a soft, sharp pencil. Mark each corner of the tracing to correspond with the corners of the map. This is to ensure your route exactly follows the road.
(vii) Finally, remember you can drive on any of the roads but not on paths or fields.

(b) In professional rallying, teams are debriefed (i.e. asked questions about their experience) after the rally. When you have completed the course, try to answer the following questions:
(i) What features of the car rally did you enjoy and why?
(ii) What features of the car rally did you find difficult? Explain why. Name any of the map skills needed that you have not yet mastered.
(iii) Suggest ways of improving the game.

CHAPTER 5

Industrial Landscapes

What can you learn from this chapter?

It can:

1 Show you parts of the industrial landscapes in South Wales
2 Help you find out about the Ordnance Survey 1:50 000 Landranger Map
3 Show you how to draw a sketch map of Swansea Bay industrial landscapes
4 Make you think about reasons for industrial location and the growth and decline of industry
5 Let you make your own decisions, choosing sites for new industry in the Swansea Bay region.

Swansea Bay industrial landscapes

Manufacturing industry involves processing raw materials to make finished or semi-finished products. Try to think of examples of this type of industry in your home area. Manufacturing industry creates a landscape that can be quite distinct from other landscapes, such as a farming or city centre landscape. One way of discovering these differences is to look at their skylines.

Activity 5:1

(a) Study Figure 5.1, which shows six skylines representing the following landscapes: city centre; farming; city suburbs; chemical industry; industrial estate; parkland. Match the landscape titles with the correct skylines.

(b) What clues helped you to identify the industrial skylines?

(c) Sketch your own skylines for part of the following landscapes: village; port; seaside town.

(d) In reality, skylines are not always so easy to identify. Sketch a skyline that is visible from your home or school, labelling the main types of landscape.

Activity 5:2

(a) The two industrial skylines that you identified in Activity 5:1(a) were drawn from two of Figures 5.2 to 5.5. Match the skylines with the correct photographs.

(b) For any two of the four photographs, write paragraphs describing the features that make them distinctive industrial landscapes.

(c) (i) If there is an industrial landscape near your home or school, go and see it, using a map as a guide. Take care as you wander around, for heavy traffic is often a feature of this landscape. Note all your impressions: the sights, sounds, smells and how you feel. Then compose a short, descriptive essay entitled 'An Industrial Landscape'. Be sure to mention your own feelings about the landscape and why you feel this way. Also, note your different reactions to different parts of the landscape. This activity will help to develop your mental image of industrial landscapes.

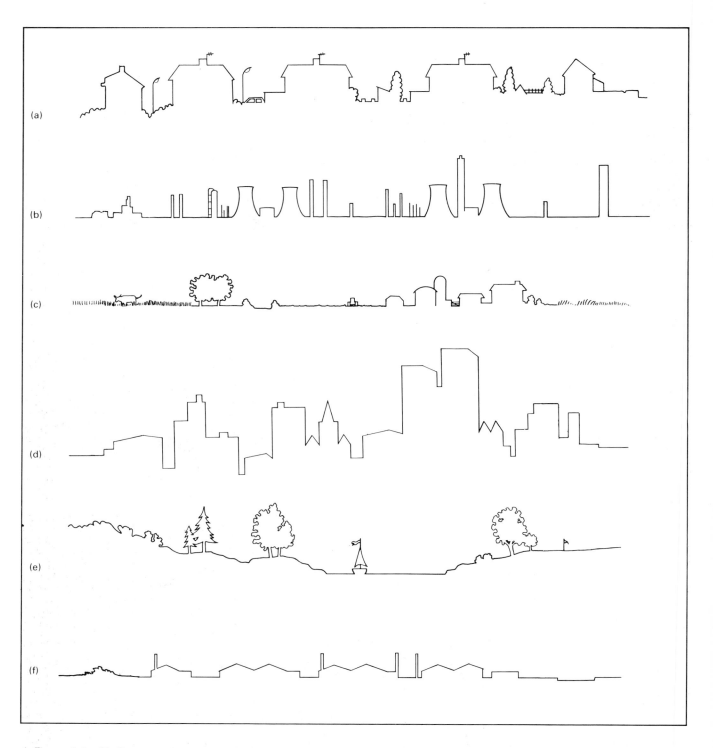

▲ Figure 5.1   Skylines

(ii) Compare the map you used and the essay you wrote in c(i), about the same industrial landscape. They are two different ways of telling people about a landscape. How do they differ? What sorts of information is each best suited to describing?
(iii) Look again at the four photographs, Figure 5.2 to Figure 5.5, and think of words that express your feelings about the industrial landscapes that they show. For example, do you find them interesting, attractive, ugly, or boring? Then think how a businessman, a housewife and an unemployed worker might view the same scenes. If you think their views may differ, say why.

▲ Figure 5.2 (above)　Industry near Swansea Bay
▼ Figure 5.4　Industry near Swansea Bay

▲ Figure 5.3 (below)　Industry near Swansea Bay
▼ Figure 5.5　Industry near Swansea Bay

Figures 5.2 to 5.5 are of industrial landscapes in the Swansea Bay region. Find Swansea, South Wales in an atlas or on a wall map. In Swansea and nearby towns there are numerous industrial areas and about 60 000 people work in them. Of these, about 30 000 work in the metal-processing industry, chiefly steel, aluminium, nickel, zinc, tinplate and titanium. The rest of the workers refine oil, manufacture car parts and chemicals or make consumer goods like food and clothes.

Activity 5:3

What kind of goods to you think are made in the industries in Figures 5.2, 5.4, and 5.5? What difficulties did you find in doing this, and why?

For another view of the Swansea Bay region, turn to Map 6 on pages 56–7, which shows part of O.S. map sheets 159 and 170. The O.S. 1:50 000 LANDRANGER MAP is a very useful, general purpose map and different from those you have seen in Chapters 1 to 4.

Activity 5:4

What major differences do you see between this type of map and the 1:25 000 map shown in Map 5?

Activity 5:5

(a) Notice the scale on the 1:50 000 Landranger Map symbols, Key 4 (page 37). What does one centimetre on a 1:50 000 map represent? (In Chapter 4 you found that one centimetre on a 1:25 000 map represents 250 metres).

(b) Bearing that in mind, what does one millimetre on a 1:50 000 map represent?

(c) Now work out in metres the length and width of the main building of the Motor Works located at 704 933.

(d) To help you understand the sizes of things on the map, draw the outline of a soccer pitch (100 × 75 metres) at the 1:50 000 scale. You will need a sharp pencil because the finished drawing will be very small. Do not forget to give your 'map' of the soccer pitch a title and scale.

(e) With the help of your teacher, find the measurements of one of your largest school buildings and draw it to the same scale.

Activity 5:6

This activity will test your ability to spot things quickly and also introduce you to some 1:50 000 map symbols. A key to these symbols is Key 4, and for the 1:25 000 map, Key 3. The challenge is to see who can beat the clock and find and write down, in less than five minutes:

(a) five symbols that are exactly the same on both 1:50 000 and 1:25 000 maps;

(b) five symbols shown only on a 1:50 000 map;

(c) five symbols shown only on a 1:25 000 map.

Mapping the industrial landscape

This chapter deals mostly with the manufacturing industry shown on Map 6.

Activity 5:7

Search Map 6 and find five examples of manufacturing industry. Write down their four-figure grid references. For example, Motor Works 70 93.

Activity 5:8

Think about the clues you used to find manufacturing industry on the map. Which of the following clues did you use?

Direct clues:
(i) large, sometimes irregularly-shaped, pink blocks;
(ii) labels such as 'works,' 'wks,' or 'Industrial Estate'.
Indirect clues:
(i) industrial areas may contain railway sidings, canals, unfenced minor roads or tracks, or be near docks, all for transporting materials in to, and goods out of, factories;

(ii) industrial areas may lie close to rivers or marshland, where land may be cheap;
(iii) nearby quarries or mines and spoil heaps or tips can provide evidence of an industry's raw material or waste products.

Did you use any other clues?

Activity 5:9

(a) To make more sense of the confusing industrial scene around Swansea Bay, you are going to draw a sketch map of the industrial landscapes. Eventually, the sketch map will contain a lot of information, so take care to draw it neatly. Place a large piece of tracing paper over the whole map (Map 6). Using colour pencils, trace the coastal outline, the rivers Tawe and Neath and the canals.

(b) Using the clues described in Activity 5:8, outline and lightly shade on the tracing all the industrial areas you can find. (Do not try to trace each individual building, but outline the areas that contain them. Try to be systematic in your search. For example, divide the map into quarters or strips and scan each thoroughly before moving on to the next quarter or strip.)

(c) Now trace the main railway lines, the M4 and all dual carriageway A roads.

(d) A list of the names of the major industries and industrial estates is given in Table 5.1. Using the grid reference, place the number of each industry or industrial estate in the correct location on the tracing. In the space occupied by the sea on your tracing, neatly list these industries and industrial estates. (Note that the B.S.C. Port Talbot steelworks extends off the map.)

(e) To complete a sketch map you must draw a frame around the map, add a key, northpoint, scale, and title: 'The Industrial Landscapes of Swansea Bay'.

Activity 5:10

Looking at the sketch map you have drawn, you could say 'many industrial areas have access to railway transport'. Write two more general statements about the location of industrial areas.

Activity 5:11

(a) Figure 5.4 shows Llandarcy Oil Refinery. The photograph was taken from an aeroplane above the point 715 954. Which direction was the photographer facing? How far is it from the cooling tower (which is at the furthest left) to the dam (which is at the right)? Roughly what distance is covered, on the ground, from the bottom of the photograph to the A48(T) bridge across the railway near the top of the photograph?

(b) Try to match the school building you drew in Activity 5:5(e) with a building of similar size in the refinery on the map. Then try to find the building in the photograph.

Table 5.1   The major industries and industrial estates of the Swansea Bay industrial landscape

Major industries

Grid Reference	Industry or Industrial Estate Number	Industry name (and product)
675 980	1	Morganite (carbon brushes) (see Figure 5.5)
667 963	2	B.S.C. Landore (steel)
662 952	3	Yorkshire Imperial Metals
602 960	4	ALCOA (aluminium)
603 964	5	IMI (titanium)
605 987	6	3 M's (tapes, adhesives)
643 000	7	B.S.C. Velindre (tinplate)
710 955	8	B.P. Llandarcy (oil refining) (see Figure 5.4)
700 932	9	Ford (gearboxes, transmissions)
735 920	10	B.P. Baglan Bay (chemicals) (see Figure 5.2)
743 964	11	Metal Box (car parts)
766 888	12	B.S.C. Port Talbot (steel)
736 934	13	Briton Ferry Works (steel) (see Figure 5.3)

Major industrial estates (I.E.)

Grid References	Industry or industrial Estate Number	Industrial Estate Name
675 975	14	Gas Works I.E. (see Figure 5.5)
685 968	15	Nantyffin/Winsh Wen I.E.
669 965	16	Plasmarl I.E.
641 947	17	Cwmdu I.E.
662 942	18	Morfa Road I.E.
624 962	19	Swansea (Fforestfach) I.E.
602 991	20	Carngoch (Gorseinon) I.E.

The British Petroleum (Baglan Bay) chemical works shown in Figure 5.2 was established here for three main reasons:
(i) It is near the source of raw materials in the oil refinery. In fact, it is connected to it by a pipeline.
(ii) There was a large area of cheap, flat land available.
(iii) The nearby railway allows finished chemical products to be sent all over Britain.

Activity 5:12

(a) Working in small groups, discuss possible reasons for the location of the industries shown in Figures 5.4 (the oil refinery), 5.5 (which shows part of the Enterprise Zone, including Morganite – to the left of the main road – and the Gas Board Industrial Estate – to the right) and 5.3 (Briton Ferry steelworks). Use photograph and map evidence to back up your ideas. You may need to refer to such factors as raw materials, market, labour supply, availability of suitable land, access to transport and so on.

(b) Still working in groups, put together two lists of information about the factors that affect industrial location. List first all the information

that is available from an O.S. 1:50 000 map – for example, nearness to transport. Second, list all the information that would help you to understand an industry's location but which cannot be found on the O.S. 1:50 000 map – for example, workers' skills.

(c) Suggest two ways in which the O.S. 1:50 000 map is useful in understanding an industrial landscape. Suggest two ways in which it is unhelpful, and say why.

New industry for old

An industrial landscape is always changing. Old factories close down while new ones are opened. The Swansea Bay industrial landscape has seen many changes over the years. From Roman times coal has been mined here and this was one reason why ironworks had been built by the 1850s. Steel, tinplate and other metals followed and Swansea became known as the 'Metal-making Centre of the World'. Most of these industries were near Swansea city centre and located very close to each other.

▼ Figure 5.6   Site of the former Briton Ferry steelworks

Nowadays, the metal industries have declined. For example, Yorkshire Imperial Metals closed with the loss of 150 jobs, B.S.C. Landore closed, losing 228 jobs, and B.S.C. Port Talbot cut 7000 people from its workforce. These losses may be softened by the creation of jobs in new industries in the suburbs or outside towns where more space is available.

Changes also happen to the pieces of the landscape that support industry. Power stations may be opened and inadequate sewage plants may be closed down. Transport links are a vital part of this support system.

Activity 5:13

Figure 5.3 shows the Briton Ferry Steelworks. It was closed in 1979 and a later photograph is shown in Figure 5.6.

(a) The site is in square 73 93. Where did the photographer stand and in which direction did he face?

(b) Suggest possible reasons why the steelworks closed.

(c) Taking note of its surroundings and its qualities, suggest ways of redeveloping the site. Give reasons to support your ideas.

Activity 5:14

(a) What are the main types of transport links shown on this map (Map 6)?

(b) List and give grid references to places where evidence of a change in the transport system can be found.

Activity 5:15

(a) Choose two industrial areas from the map, one which might be old and the other which might be new. Give reasons for your choice.

(b) 'Brainstorming' is a useful way of producing ideas. Working in groups, the object is to think up as many ideas as possible, however unlikely they may seem. Do not criticise other people's ideas but try to build on them. Keep a record of your group ideas. Using this technique, suggest as many reasons as possible why:
(i) industries close down;
(ii) industries may change location;
(iii) new industries are set up.

(c) Give reasons why a factory owner, looking for a site for a new factory, might be attracted to the Swansea Bay region. Quote map evidence where possible to back up your answers.

Swansea Centre for
Trade and Industry

For information and assistance in the commercial and industrial development of Swansea

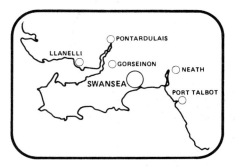

The City of Swansea lies at the heart of the wider conurbation, with a population of 500,000 within a 10-mile radius and an experienced industrial workforce of 220,000 - that is Swansea Bay City. The M4 links Swansea Bay City direct with London, supplementing the regular British Rail High-Speed services giving easy communications between the City and the whole of the Southern United Kindom.

▲ Figure 5.7   A 1981 newspaper advertisement

Activity 5:16

The Swansea City Council competes with other councils across the country to attract new industry. One important reason for this is to create new jobs. In February 1981, about 14 000 people were unemployed in Swansea and nearby Morriston.

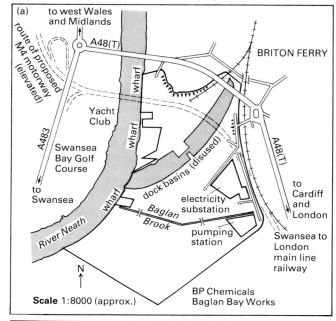

(a) Figure 5.7 shows a newspaper advertisement designed to attract industry. If you wanted to build a new factory, what features of the advertisement might interest you?

(b) What further information about the Swansea Bay region would be useful to a factory owner if he/she was interested in opening a new factory there?

(c) Make up your own advertisement like the one in Figure 5.7. From Map 6, choose more information that might attract a factory owner. For example, see evidence at: 67 92, 599 906, and 630 920.

(d) Swansea Bay competes with other regions in Britain for new industry. The site shown in Figure 5.6 is now the Briton Ferry Industrial Estate. A map of the estate and a sketch of what it may look like in the future are shown in Figure 5.8.
(i) What things might a factory owner find attractive in Figure 5.8, and why?
(ii) What kind of image do you think Figure 5.8 is trying to convey of the industrial estate of the future?

Figure 5.8   Briton Ferry Industrial Estate:
◀ (a) a map of the site, ▼ (b) an artist's impression

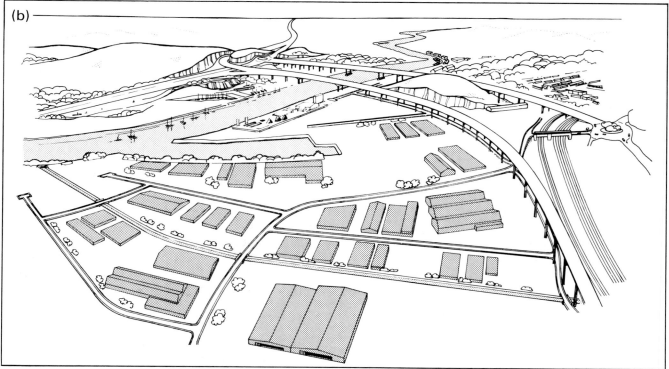

(e) Collect more examples of these types of advertisements from newspapers or magazines. List the different sorts of information that each one includes.

(f) Suppose your home region, or an industrial site near you, wanted to encourage new businesses. Design an advertisement pointing out the features that a factory owner might find attractive.

The Swansea Centre for Trade and Industry put the advertisement, Figure 5.7, in the newspaper. They send a package of information to any factory owner who is interested enough to write to them. The main points in this package are listed below.

Main Points of the Information Package
1 West Glamorgan has good farming land. There is plenty of very attractive recreational land, especially in the Gower Peninsula (which is west of Swansea).
2 The climate is mild.
3 There are excellent road and rail links and Swansea Airport is just 9 kilometres west of Swansea city centre. It handles businesspeople's flights, while Cardiff International Airport is only 40 minutes drive to the east. Both Swansea port and Port Talbot are tidal. Port Talbot can handle deep water boats.
4 Many successful international firms have located their businesses in the Swansea region. They make a very wide range of goods.
5 The University College, Swansea (629 920) has important links with industry through industrial research and the training of specialist workers. There are many opportunities elsewhere in the region for training industrial workers.
6 There is a wide variety of skilled, semi-skilled, professional, technical and office workers available. The road and bus network make it easy for them to travel over the whole region.
7 Housing is cheap and there are plenty of good shops.
8 There is a great amount of Government help for new industry.
9 A large number of industrial sites are available for development.

Activity 5:17

(a) If you were a factory owner looking for somewhere in Britain to open a new factory, and you had sent for the package from the Swansea region, you would read the following: 'attractive recreational land', 'successful international firms', 'opportunities for training'.

Why are each of these features listed in the package?

(b) Government help for industry is very important nowadays. There are four zones in the region with differing amounts of Government help available. These zones are briefly described as follows:

Zones of Government help for industry
Zone I – Intermediate Area The *help available* is Government money for building new factories and for some removal costs. The *zone boundaries* include nearly all the land west of the Urban District Council Boundary line, which runs roughly northward from 700 912. The exception is the Zone IV area.
Zone II – Development Area The *help available* is the same as in Zone I. Also help is available for buying machinery and employing workers. The *zone boundaries* include all the land between the boundary in Zone I and the Urban District Council Boundary line, which runs roughly north-east and east from 721 911.
Zone III – Special Development Area The *help available* is the same type as in Zones I and II but includes even more money. The *zone boundaries* include all the land south and east of the Urban District Council Boundary line, which starts at 721 911.
Zone IV – Enterprise Zone The *help available* consists of all the benefits of the Intermediate Area plus lower taxes. To get building plans approved usually takes a long time. In this zone red tape has been cut and a factory could be started in a month. The *zone boundaries* are harder to trace. The boundaries are: The River Tawe from 674 979 to 663 958; the railway from 663 958 to 683 969; a line roughly northwards from 683 969 to 687 990; the railway from 687 990 to 683 991; and the road from 683 991 to 674 979.

Draw the zone boundaries on your tracing of the map. Label each zone with its title.

Industrial adviser

Three companies, based somewhere else in Britain and in the USA, have decided to open new factories in the Swansea Bay region. Now they have to choose factory sites that could best satisfy their needs. A description of these needs is provided in the three company profiles, as follows.

Profile: Company A

This Californian company wants to build its major European factory in the Swansea Bay region. It will make silicon chips to fit many types of electronic goods from calculators to televisions. The Swansea factory will concentrate on making large amounts of identical chips in a process that will be quiet and clean.

Collection of raw materials: Two lorry loads per week will be brought from suppliers in the Midlands.

Processing of raw materials: This company wants to start production as soon as possible. Therefore, a ready-made factory is preferred. The *site* can be as small as one-half hectare, but two hectares will allow for future growth. The *labour* needed is 150, and later 300, workers, of which 25 per cent will be highly skilled. The need for *power and services*, such as electricity, water and waste disposal, will be small. *Machinery* is in the form of specialised electronic assembly and testing equipment.

Distribution of finished product: The silicon chips have a small bulk but a high value. Rapid, efficient distribution in this competitive industry is important. Fifty per cent of the production will be sold in the North, Midlands and South East England, and distribution can be by a small van or car or by rail. The other 50 per cent is to be sold abroad in Europe and the USA.

Profile: Company B

This company will make small amounts of dangerous chemicals to be used in other industries.

Collection of raw materials: The raw material chemicals will be brought from any major chemical works by rail tanker (20 loads per week) or road tanker (40 loads per week) or by pipe if the works are close.

Processing of raw materials: Company B wants five to ten hectares of level ground, on a *site* which must be at least 500 metres from the nearest housing. The *labour* needed is 250 workers, of which most will be skilled and highly skilled. *Power and services*, such as electricity and water, will be needed in moderate amounts. Waste disposal is handled by another specialist firm, which must have access for its vehicles from a main road. The *machinery* is in the form of very specialised equipment.

Distribution of finished product: Of the 10 rail tanker loads (or 20 road tanker loads) of goods produced each week, about 50 per cent goes to the tinplate works at grid reference 643 000. Of the remainder, small quantities are sold to several firms in the Lower Swansea Valley area and to the east in Cardiff.

Profile: Company C

Company C is a large soft drinks firm located near London, that wishes to open a warehouse in the Swansea region in order to supply a large local market. The warehouse would be a receiving place, a store and a centre for distribution.

Collection of raw materials: Collection of ready-made and bottled soft drinks will be made by 40 lorry loads a week from London, returning along the M4 motorway.

Processing of raw materials: A one-hectare *site* with a ready-made factory is preferred, but the company is willing to build if necessary. They need a *labour* force of 20 unskilled workers. The *power and services* required are small amounts of electricity, water and waste disposal. Only a few *machines*, such as forklift trucks, are needed.

Distribution of finished product: The market consists of numerous shops, pubs, hotels, etc. which are spread throughout the area shown on the map. Distribution is carried out by a dozen delivery vans.

Activity 5:18

(a) A description of factory sites available in the Swansea Bay region is given in Table 5.2 (on pages 72–3). Mark each of these sites (a–h) in its correct place on your tracing of Swansea Bay's industrial landscapes.

(b) Some of the spaces in columns 4 to 8 in Table 5.2 have been left blank. Using information from your tracing and Map 6, fill in these spaces on a copy of the table. You may like to work in small teams with each member concentrating on finding out things about one or two sites.

(c) You now have a great deal of information about the area and the factory sites. Your task is to act as an Industrial Adviser and to choose the best site for each company. Try to consider all the features of each site and all the points about each firm. Remember the choice may not be easy. After making your decision, write three brief reports to use in a class discussion, explaining the reasons for your choices.

(d) Choose one of the three companies and suggest its likely impact on the community near your chosen site.

(e) What kinds of information would have made your choice easier?

(f) Imagine that these three companies described above were to be sited in your home region. Study an O.S. 1:50 000 or 1:25 000 map of your home region and choose suitable sites for them. You might like to improve your judgement of each site by visiting them to make more detailed notes on such things as: suitability of the roads and the amount of congestion, state of the building site (whether it is ready to build on or not), whether there are bus stops or railway stations nearby.

Table 5.2 Factory sites available in the Swansea Bay region

1 Factory sites available (grid reference)	2 Site size (hectares)	3 Site condition	4 Approximate distance along roads from nearest motorway junction (km)	5 Approximate distance along roads from nearest station or railway sidings (km)
a Gas Works Industrial Estate (I.E.) (675975)	1.5	Flat land, close to river but protected from flooding (see figure 5.4)	2.0	on site
b Carngoch (Gorseinon) I.E. (602991)	8.0	Open land, sloping slightly west. Much is still green fields	2.2	1.0
c Winsh-Wen I.E. (685968)	10.0	Prepared sites up to 5 ha in size in young woodland setting	2.4	0.2
d Briton Ferry I.E. (S.E. corner of 7393)	50.0	Cleared site of former steelworks. Being prepared for use. See Figures 5.6 & 5.8. Sites up to 25 ha available.		
e Swansea Docks (6792)	45.0	Sites of all sizes up to 15.0 ha available		
f Neath Abbey Industrial Site (734972)	11.0	Flat, low-lying site. Needs flood protection work		
g Purcell Avenue, Sandfields (734913)	11.0	Flat, prepared sites up to 4.0 ha		
h Swansea I.E. (Fforestfach) (624962)	23.0	Well established sites. Various sizes up to 10 ha		

6 Land uses surrounding site	7 Form of Government help available (e.g. Enterprise Zone, Development Area etc.)	8 General comments
Farmland, derelict land, some housing, other industry	Enterprise Zone	Part of an established industrial area. Three separate sites available, each 0.5 ha. One of these was a ready-made factory
Farmland, industry	Intermediate Area	Land in process of adaptation to industrial use and will be available in six months time
Woodland, railway, industry	Intermediate Area	Light and general industrial use only
		Access to sea is possible from site. Deep water port 4 km
		Land on dockside freed from previous dock use
		Two ready-made factories each 0.5 ha
		Several ready-made factories (0.3–2.0 ha) available

CHAPTER 6

A Landscape of Leisure

What can you learn from this chapter?

It can:

1 Suggest how an O.S. 1:50 000 map might be used for planning personal leisure activities
2 Indicate ways in which park recreation can be planned on a broad scale using the same map
3 Show how detailed recreation planning on a local scale involves thinking about the users, as well as the landscape

Relax with a map

The weekend brings with it opportunities for relaxation and recreation. To some this means the chance to take part in a sporting activity, to others quite the opposite. They may like nothing better than to sit in the sun and read their newspaper.

Often the need to relax in these ways results in journeys to new places. The Ordnance Survey Landranger Map, Map 7 (page 58), contains useful information that can help people discover the possibilities for recreation and tourism in the countryside. The following activity suggests ways in which the map can be used.

Activity 6:1

(a) Imagine that you have just moved to a new house in Harefield (05 90) and some relatives have come to stay for the weekend. On the Saturday everyone wants to do different things. Even though you do not know the area well, it is your job to use the map and give six-figure grid references to places where people might be able to take part in the following activities:
(i)   outdoor swimming;
(ii) kite flying;
(iii) train spotting;
(iv) bird watching;
(v) sunbathing.

(b) Suggest three extra pieces of information, not found on the map, that would help you to decide where to go.

(c) Although everyone wants to do different things, give the six-figure grid reference of one place that allows you to do the largest combination of these activities.

Activity 6:2

(a) On the Sunday, your family and other relatives decide they want an afternoon out, exploring the local area. The O.S. 1:50 000 map can help you with this problem, too. Plan a route for a short drive, for two cars, of not more than 25 kilometres, which includes several places which should interest your relatives. This can be done by tracing the route and stopping places from the map. Label your route neatly and give it a suitable title. Try to avoid driving along the same road twice.

(b) Compare your route with your neighbour's. To what extent have you planned similar routes?

Park planning

Map 7 (on page 58) shows an area on the fringe of north-west London. It is quite likely that on a pleasant, sunny Sunday afternoon, some of the other 4.75 million people who live within 25 kilometres of the edge of the map will want to use local leisure facilities too! To cope with this great demand for spare-time activities, local councils have built recreation centres inside the towns. What have they done to help increase the use of the countryside for leisure?

Have you spotted the two Country Parks on the map extract? Country Parks are usually small, being less than five square kilometres in size. They are positioned close to towns. Regional Parks are larger and they may include Country Parks inside their boundaries. The proposed Colne Valley Regional Park runs north to south through the centre of the map. Larger still are the National Parks, which cover hundreds of square kilometres. They are mostly found in upland areas of north and west Britain.

The aims of the Colne Valley Regional Park are to keep it, as far as possible, rural in nature, so that it is an attractive place for peaceful leisure activities, such as fishing, picnicking and swimming. At the same time, wildlife is to be protected, pollution minimised, and the way people use the land is to be controlled. Lastly, the Park aims to stop further spreading of towns. Important features of the Park are its activity centres for use by large numbers of people.

Activity 6:3

The sketch map, Figure 6.1, shows the northern half of the Park.

(a) Part of the Park in the top right corner of Figure 6.1 has been left blank. How do you think this area might be zoned for use? On a copy of Figure 6.1, use the key to add the symbols for:
(i) a largely agricultural area;
(ii) an area of woods;
(iii) a built-up area;
(iv) a possible wildlife sanctuary;
(v) a major footpath.
Study the O.S. 1:50 000 map, Map 7, to help you to decide these land uses.

(b) (i) Give three reasons to explain why drawing a boundary around the Park presents problems.
(ii) Using both Map 7 and Figure 6.1 look closely at the park boundary between 009 911 and 018 923. Which natural and man-made features have been chosen as the park boundary line? Explain why you think these features were chosen.

(c) Three activity centres have been left off Figure 6.1: x concentrates on sailing, boating and fishing; y has facilities for golf and flying of light aircraft; z is a nature reserve and can cater for riding, camping and fishing. Where could these three centres be located? Study Map 7 for the kind of landscape features that will support these activities. Add them to your copy of Figure 6.1, using appropriate symbols. Then explain why you chose these locations.

(d) Plan a circular walk of between three and six kilometres, somewhere in the Colne Valley Regional Park. Design a leaflet to advertise the walk, in which you should include a sketch map of the route, a description of what might be seen and some directions on how to reach the beginning of the walk.

Activity 6:4

(a) Imagine that you are in control of planning the park and that Government thinking has changed. You have been told to reduce its area. On another copy of Figure 6.1, design a new park, using only 25 square kilometres. This means making some hard decisions. You have to decide which features are essential to your park, whether it should remain as one unit or be split into separate pieces, and which areas might have most need for this Park. When you have chosen 25 squares, carefully select a boundary line and draw it on your map. Write a short paragraph as the introduction to a leaflet entitled, 'The New Colne Valley Regional Park', explaining your decisions.

(b) Compare the parks designed by your class. How has the character of the Park changed? Which people have chosen to emphasise one aspect of the Park at the expense of another, and why? Let a class vote decide which five best designs should receive Landscape Awards.

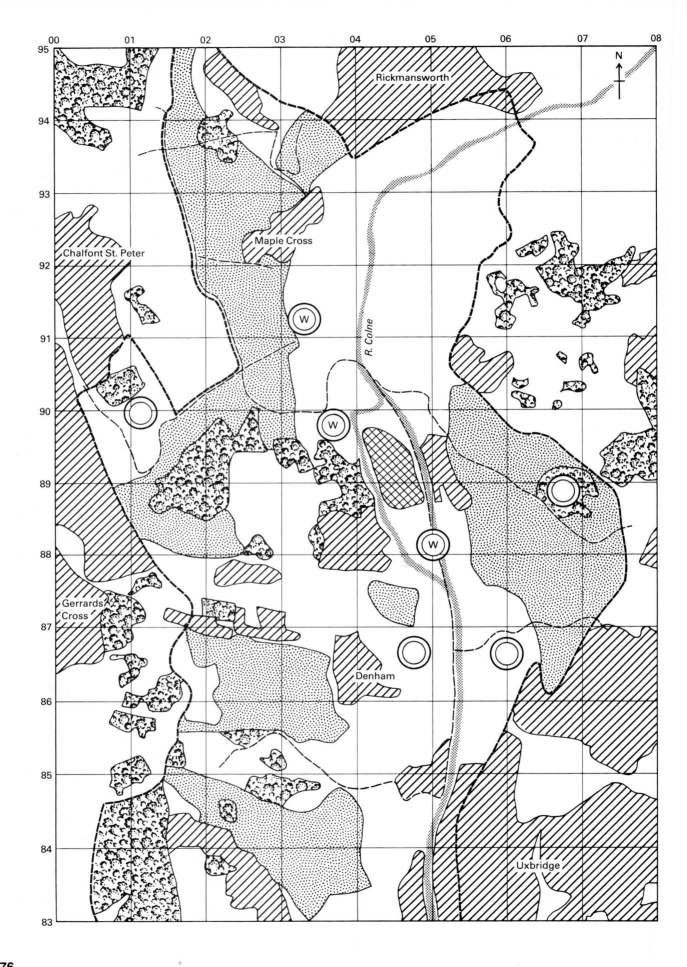

Activity 6:5

In most parks there are problems to be solved. Some features within the Colne Valley Regional Park are in conflict with the aims outlined earlier in this chapter. For example, there are several sources of noise and examples of unsightly features, which can be identified on Map 7.

(a) Use different colours to mark on your copy of Figure 6.1 various aspects of the landscape that are likely to cause noise pollution.

(b) Make a list of landscape features that are unsightly and then try to find examples of them on the map. Use another colour to mark them on your copy of Figure 6.1.

(c) Suggest ways of solving these pollution problems.

(d) The A405 (T) road at present ends in square 03 93. Draw a sketch map to indicate a possible route southwards to link the roundabout at 032 942 on the A405 (T) with the M40, which ends at 048 858. Add notes to the map to explain your choice of route.

◀ Figure 6.1   The northern half of the Colne Valley Regional Park

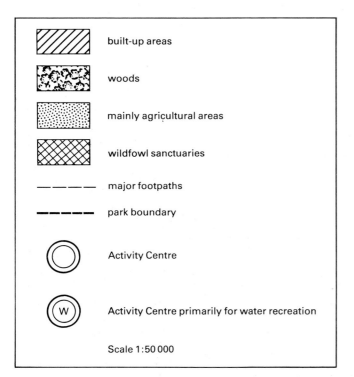

	built-up areas
	woods
	mainly agricultural areas
	wildfowl sanctuaries
– – – –	major footpaths
▬ ▬ ▬	park boundary
◎	Activity Centre
Ⓦ	Activity Centre primarily for water recreation

Scale 1:50 000

Three lakes

The proposed Colne Valley Regional Park shows how we need to plan the 'landscape of leisure' on a broad scale. The planning does not stop with the choice of a suitable region. Detailed studies and plans have to be made of the smallest sections of that region. This will involve the ideas that you came up with in Park Planning, as well as asking for new ideas and thoughts that are appropriate to the different scale.

Activity 6:6

Study the aerial photograph, Figure 6.2, which was taken over 043 930.

(a) In which direction was the camera facing?

(b) The furthest lake is called Batchworth Lake and it contains two wooded islands not shown on the map. The next lake is Bury Lake. Name the nearest lake, the canal and the river.

The area shown on the photograph is the leisure landscape chosen for detailed study in this chapter. The recreational use of these lakes presents an interesting planning problem for you to solve.

Activity 6:7

(a) (i) Read the following piece of background information. Find the places and features that it refers to on Figure 6.3.
(ii) Read through the list of leisure activities that follows the background information.
(iii) Your job is to use this information to decide where each activity can best take place, on and around the lakes. Place a piece of tracing paper over Figure 6.3 and mark your own symbol for each activity on the tracing, in the places that you think are the most appropriate.

(b) Write a brief report, giving reasons for your plan. Be prepared to explain your decisions to the local council (i.e. the rest of your class!).

▲ Figure 6.2 Aerial photograph of three Colne Valley lakes

▼ Figure 6.3 The three lakes and their surrounding land use

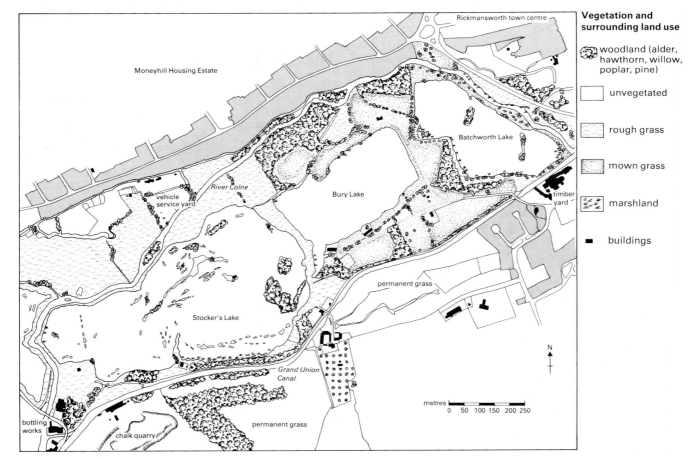

Background information

Geology: The River Colne has cut a broad valley, 60 metres deep, through low chalk hills. The gravels covering the valley floor have been quarried, though working finished in 1920. Nowadays, water fills the hollows left behind, creating lakes.

Water: Batchworth is about four metres deep, though there are shallows around the edge. Bury Lake is deeper, with no shallows except for a gently sloping eastern shoreline. Stocker's Lake has numerous shallows and islands. The water in all three lakes is clean, though Stocker's Lake is especially pure.

Climate: Batchworth tends to be sheltered from breezes. All lakes get plenty of sun.

Vegetation and wildlife: The grass around Batchworth and Bury Lakes is mown regularly. It will last for a long time under a lot of tramping feet. There is very rough grass around Stocker's Lake. There are plenty of mature trees round all lakes. Reedy patches fringe part of Batchworth Lake, which has a variety of fish. Stocker's Lake has the greatest assortment of plant, bird and fish life.

Ownership: The local council owns Batchworth and Bury Lakes and the land surrounding them. Stocker's Lake, and the land around it, is owned by the local water authority.

Access: Vehicle access to all lakes is via a bridge and road just south of Batchworth Lake. Pedestrian access is either the same way, or via a footbridge just north of Batchworth Lake.

Non-Recreational land uses: Water is taken from the gravels under Stocker's Lake to increase local water supply and the water authority do not want the water polluted in any way.

Leisure activities

Private fishing: An airline company wants exclusive fishing rights to a lake for its workers. It can afford to buy those rights.

Public fishing: There is a local demand for fishing facilities for the general public.

Sailing: A group of local schools need access to a lake during the week. On Sundays, a small private sailing club also needs access.

Swimming: Sunny days could attract large crowds of people for outdoor swimming.

General recreation: Open space, on land, is in great demand for such things as sunbathing, picnicking and walking dogs. You need to allow a large space, say 100 metres by 100 metres, for a car park.

Bird watching: Bird watchers want peace and quiet, a general lack of people and a variety of birdlife.

Zones in space and time

This may sound like the title of a science fiction film, but it is merely the way that the local authority solves the problem of different activities sharing the same resources. Batchworth and Bury Lakes are known as Rickmansworth Aquadrome and they have, in fact, been used for recreation since 1929.

Activity 6:8

(a) Study Figure 6.4, which shows how the lakes have been zoned for use throughout the year. Using your copy or tracing from Activity 6:7, with colours or hatching, shade the areas used by each leisure activity in the Aquadrome. Do this only for the month of July.

(b) In what ways does the actual plan differ from the plan you chose in Activity 6:7(a)?

(c) Give some reasons to explain why different activities can be zoned for the same area.

(d) How would you change the zoning system to allow access to:
(i) a local sub-aqua club;
(ii) tiny children who want to use the Aquadrome for paddling;
(iii) a water skiing club?

The space and time zones show what activities have been made available. An important issue, however, is how much use is made of the facilities.

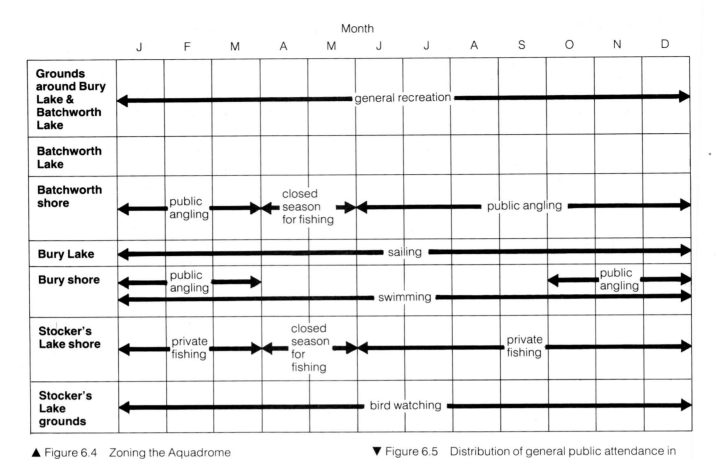

▲ Figure 6.4   Zoning the Aquadrome

▼ Figure 6.5   Distribution of general public attendance in one summer

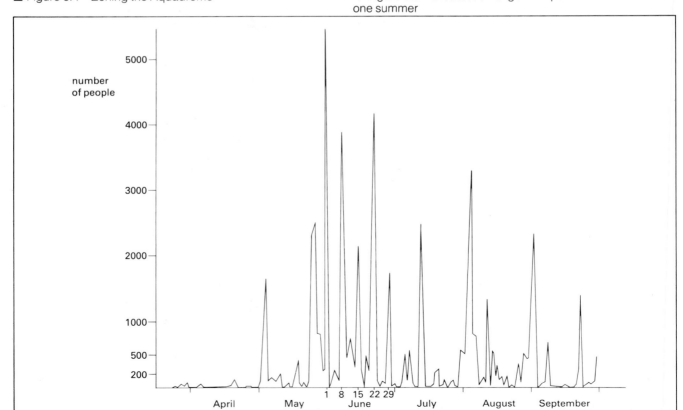

Activity 6:9

(a) Figure 6.5 shows the total number of people using the Aquadrome (excluding Stocker's Lake) each day in one particular summer.

(i) How many times did the attendance exceed 1000 people?

(ii) Try to work out, to the nearest hundred, how many people were there on each of the following days of June: 1st, 8th, 15th, 22nd and 29th.

(iii) What days of the week do you think these were? Explain your answer.

(iv) Suggest reasons why, even on these days, the attendance varied so much.

(v) What was the highest attendance in April? Give a possible reason to explain why this was so.

(b) Suggest ways in which the pattern might vary from year to year.

(c) Write down at least four general conclusions that you can draw from the graph, about the numbers of people using the Aquadrome.

(d) The great variation in daily attendance figures might cause some problems. What do you think they might be?

(e) Design a small advertisement for the local newspaper to attract more people to use the Aquadrome at off-peak times.

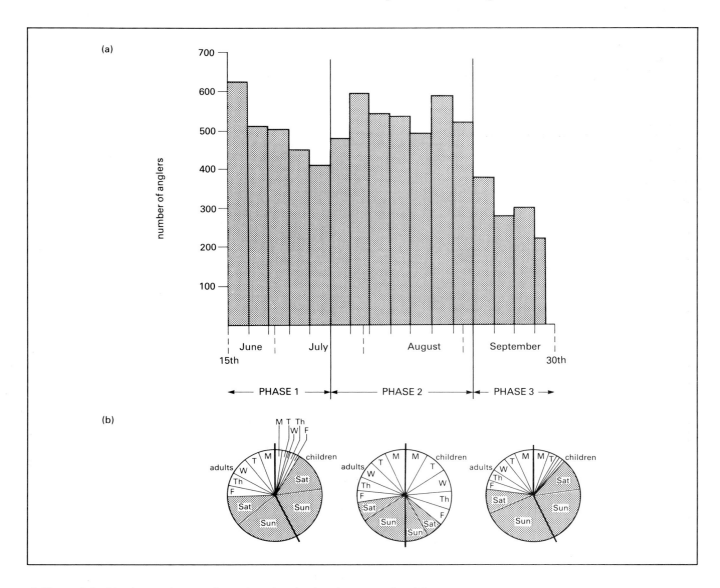

▲ Figure 6.6   Number and proportions of anglers for the sixteen weeks of the summer season

Activity 6:10

The anglers using Batchworth Lake contrast in many ways with the general public. Their fishing season starts on June 15th, and the weekly attendance averages are shown in Figure 6.6(a). It has been divided into three time phases, and pie charts have been added in Figure 6.6(b). The pie charts show the average proportions of adults and children for each day of the week. For each phase of use by the anglers, write two sentences to say what the block graph and associated pie chart show. Write down reasons to explain the variation in the diagrams.

In one particular summer, the leaders of each group of people using Rickmansworth Aquadrome were asked questions about themselves. Some of the results are shown in Figure 6.7.

Activity 6:11

(a) (i) Who would seem to you to be the average user of Rickmansworth Aquadrome? Write two sentences describing the average user.
(ii) From the information given in Figure 6.7, write two sentences describing the average angler who uses the Aquadrome.

(b) Suggest two dangers and two advantages of describing the public in terms of averages.

Figure 6.7   Questionnaire survey results ▶

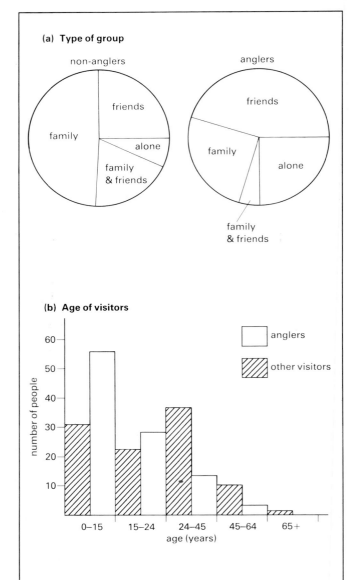

(a) **Type of group**

(b) **Age of visitors**

(c) **Activities which users took part in**		%	(Anglers)
sunbathing		59	(1)
swimming		54	(2)
picnicking		33	(4)
playing with children		38	(1)
reading, sleeping		30	(3)
watching water sports		17	(0)
angling		15	(100)
boating		14	(1)
walking dog		9	(1)

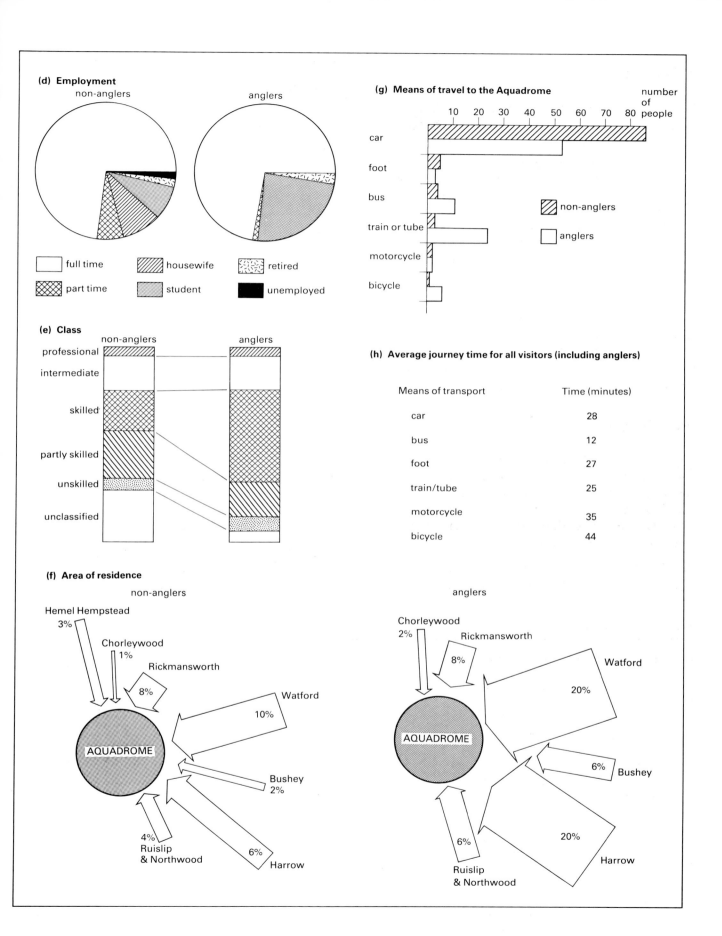

(d) Employment

non-anglers　　anglers

- full time
- housewife
- retired
- part time
- student
- unemployed

(g) Means of travel to the Aquadrome

number of people

10　20　30　40　50　60　70　80

- car
- foot
- bus
- train or tube
- motorcycle
- bicycle

non-anglers

anglers

(e) Class

non-anglers　　anglers

- professional
- intermediate
- skilled
- partly skilled
- unskilled
- unclassified

(h) Average journey time for all visitors (including anglers)

Means of transport	Time (minutes)
car	28
bus	12
foot	27
train/tube	25
motorcycle	35
bicycle	44

(f) Area of residence

non-anglers

- Hemel Hempstead 3%
- Chorleywood 1%
- Rickmansworth 8%
- Watford 10%
- Bushey 2%
- Ruislip & Northwood 4%
- Harrow 6%

AQUADROME

anglers

- Chorleywood 2%
- Rickmansworth 8%
- Watford 20%
- Bushey 6%
- Ruislip & Northwood 6%
- Harrow 20%

AQUADROME

Activity 6:12

(a) Look at the photograph, Figure 6.8, taken at the extreme eastern corner of Bury Lake, looking northwards. Make a list of the things that the people are doing.

(b) Compare your list with the things that people said they were doing in Figure 6.7(c). Think of two headings, one for the group of activities taking place in the photograph and another for the list of activities that the rest of the people said they were doing in Figure 6.7(c).

(c) How many of these activities could be done at home, assuming that the people each have a garden?

To get a clear picture of where people were inside the Aquadrome, a very accurate count of people was made at 4.00 p.m. on an August Bank Holiday. As the day was cloudy, only 1068 people came all day. This was lower than most busy Sundays. But it gave a good picture of where people were at that one instant in time. The results are shown in the dispersion map, Figure 6.9.

Activity 6:13

(a) Describe the distribution shown in Figure 6.9, saying where there are high, medium and low densities of people. Make clear in your description the differences in distribution of each of the four types of user.

(b) Suppose you were the manager of the Aquadrome and you wished to get extra funds from the local council for improvements to the facilities. Use Figure 6.9 as the basis for a written proposal to persuade the council members to give you the extra money. Explain the location of different users, saying where facilities for them seem to be adequate. Then highlight the possible problem areas and make suggestions as to how the problems might be solved.

Future issues

Over time, people's leisure interests may change, and it is a very sensible thing to try to spot the problems before they happen. One way of doing this is to discuss 'what should we do if . . .?'

Policy, or future planning, for the Aquadrome is decided by a committee on the local council. They can be influenced by the good arguments of any group of users.

▼ Figure 6.8   Recreation at Bury Lake shore

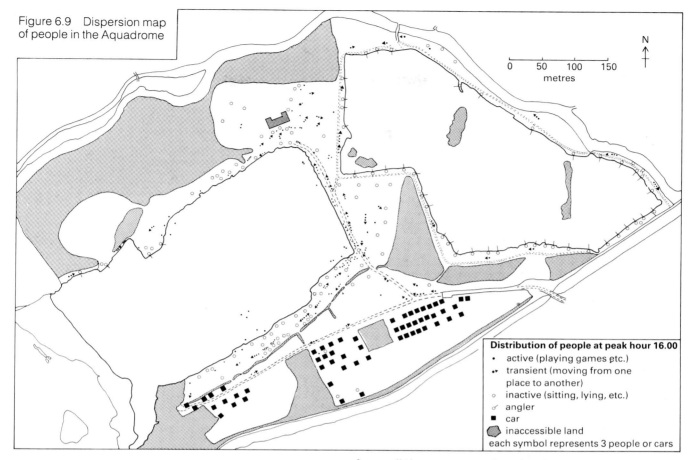

Figure 6.9 Dispersion map of people in the Aquadrome

Distribution of people at peak hour 16.00
- · active (playing games etc.)
- ·► transient (moving from one place to another)
- ○ inactive (sitting, lying, etc.)
- ⚲ angler
- ■ car
- ▨ inaccessible land

each symbol represents 3 people or cars

Activity 6:14

In this activity there are two issues to be discussed. They are outlined below. Your class will be divided into six groups, also listed below. Your aim is to prepare solutions to the problems each issue contains. Each group must make sure that it makes a strong case for itself in any proposed solution.

The six groups can put forward their solutions at a meeting of all the groups. The meeting will be chaired by your teacher, who will act as a member of the local council. At the end of the discussion, the groups can choose the best three solutions by taking a vote.

The issues

Stocker's Lake changes hands: The water authority no longer needs its water supply from the boreholes next to Stocker's Lake. It has sold the lake and the adjoining land to the local council so that all the lakes come under the same ownership. The exclusive fishing rights have expired. There has been an increasing demand from all the groups using the Aquadrome for water and land facilities.

Rising tide of demand: New local housing estates, better road transport and increased unemployment have placed the Aquadrome under great pressure. Batchworth Lake is overfished; there are long waiting lists to join the private sailing club; the lakeside banks and the grassy areas are becoming eroded by the increasing numbers of people.

The groups

1 *The Private Fishing Club* using Stocker's Lake at present sends four representatives (out of a class of 30).
2 *The General Public Fishermen* are represented by six people.
3 *The General Public*, including swimmers, picnickers, etc., sends seven people.
4 *The Hertfordshire Schools Sailing Club* has three representatives.
5 *The Colne Sailing Club* has five representatives.
6 *The Bird Watchers* have five people at the meeting.

CHAPTER 7

A Transport Landscape

Sugar on the move

Did you sprinkle sugar on your breakfast cereal this morning, or stir sugar into your tea or coffee? Try to think of all the products you have used, over the last day, that contain sugar. The sugar you eat is made either from sugar cane or from sugar beet. Sugar cane is a grass-like plant that grows only in the tropics. Sugar beet looks like a large, fat parsnip (see Figure 7.1) and it can grow in the British climate.

Growing and harvesting sugar beet means using lots of machines, as seen in Figure 7.2, and British farmers deliver their own loads to the factories (Figure 7.3). An aerial photograph of the British Sugar Corporation's sugar beet factory at Peterborough is shown in Figure 7.4. The raw sugar beet is stored for a short while before going on the move again (Figure 7.5). Inside the factory, sugar beet is cleaned and sliced before the sugar is extracted in hot water. This sugar solution is purified in evaporators, Figure 7.6, before being dried and either packed in the familiar sugar packets or stored in huge silos, like those seen on the left side of Figure 7.4, for bulk delivery. Figure 7.7 shows a bulk tanker loaded with 20 tonnes of refined sugar for delivery to a cake-making firm. Fifty-five per cent of British Sugar Corporation's production goes to the food and drink industry and forty-five per cent to shops.

▲ Figure 7.1   A sugar beet

▲ Figure 7.2   Harvesting sugar beet

▲ Figure 7.3   Delivering sugar beet

▲ Figure 7.4   British Sugar Corporation sugar beet factory, Peterborough

▲ Figure 7.5   Storage and transport of sugar beet in a factory

▲ Figure 7.6   Evaporators inside a sugar beet factory

▲ Figure 7.7   Twenty tonne bulk delivery road tanker

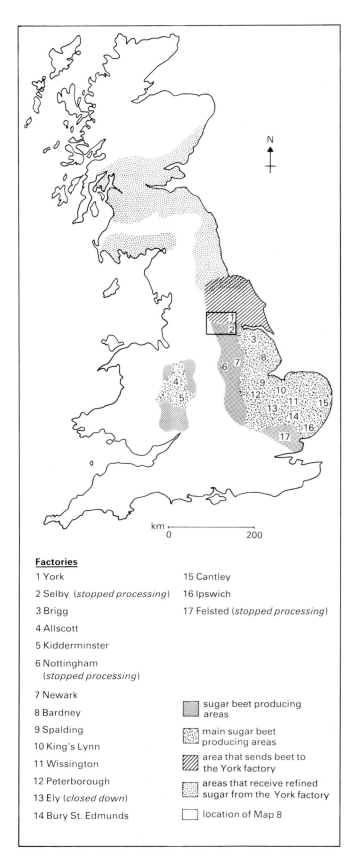

Factories

1 York	15 Cantley
2 Selby *(stopped processing)*	16 Ipswich
3 Brigg	17 Felsted *(stopped processing)*
4 Allscott	
5 Kidderminster	
6 Nottingham *(stopped processing)*	
7 Newark	
8 Bardney	
9 Spalding	
10 King's Lynn	
11 Wissington	
12 Peterborough	
13 Ely *(closed down)*	
14 Bury St. Edmunds	

- sugar beet producing areas
- main sugar beet producing areas
- area that sends beet to the York factory
- areas that receive refined sugar from the York factory
- location of Map 8

▲ Figure 7.8   The sugar beet industry in Britain

Activity 7:1

(a) To show clearly this whole process from field to food, draw a FLOW DIAGRAM to illustrate what happens at each stage. That is, draw a set of boxes, linked by arrows showing the direction of movement of the sugar beet and sugar. In each box draw a symbol, perhaps based on the photographs, to represent what is happening. Label each part of the process.

(b) You may have noticed that, at each stage of sugar beet and sugar movement, different transport is used. Label these transport types on your flow diagram.

(c) On a piece of tracing paper placed over Figure 7.4, use arrows to indicate the possible direction of flow of sugar beet into the Peterborough factory. Then show the flow of sugar through and out of the factory.

(d) In Chapter 5 you identified different industrial landscapes. In your own words, try to describe the industrial landscape shown in Figure 7.4.

In Chapter 5 you also studied some of the reasons for the location of industry. You can see the location of all the British Sugar Corporation's sugar beet processing factories in Britain, including Peterborough, in Figure 7.8.

Activity 7:2

(a) Describe the location of these factories.

(b) Suggest possible reasons to explain the location of the factories.

(c) The last few years have seen changes in the area of land under sugar beet and in the total production of refined sugar from British Sugar Corporation. Draw two graphs of the figures shown in Table 7.1 and say what they show. Why do you think home production has changed and what advantages and disadvantages do these changes bring?

(d) Look closely now at the factory at York, in Figure 7.8. What differences do you notice about the area that supplies York with sugar beet and the areas York supplies with refined sugar?

Table 7.1 Sugar beet area and sugar production

(a) Total area on which sugar beet was grown

Year	Area (hectares)
1974–75	182 000
1975–76	193 000
1976–77	201 000
1977–78	not available
1978–79	204 000
1979–80	213 000

(b) Total sugar production by BSC

Year	Amount produced (tonnes) per year
1975	568 000
1976	641 000
1977	695 000
1978	950 000
1979	1 022 000
1980	1 154 000

The British Sugar Corporation's fleet of 200 bulk tankers takes the sugar, in either solid or liquid form, across the whole of Britain. All of the British crop of sugar beet is harvested and processed in October, November, December and January of each year. This hectic period is called the 'campaign', when time is precious because the crop must be processed before it rots. To save wasting time and money, Ed Badley, in the British Sugar Corporation's transport planning department, carefully works out the movement of the refined sugar.

Tackling the problem

The task you face is an actual problem, chosen from those that Ed Badley has to solve every day.

Activity 7:3

(a) You have to plan the best route for a 20 tonne bulk delivery of sugar from the York factory to Better Bake Ltd in Halifax. To help you to do this, the relevant part of the O.S. 1:250 000 Routemaster Map is shown in Map 8 on page 99. The key is Key 2B (page 35). On these maps, four centimetres represents ten kilometres on the ground. List other differences between this map and the 1:50 000 map, used in Chapters 5 and 6.

(b) Place a piece of tracing paper over the map, Map 8, and mark on it the location of the York factory and Better Bake Ltd, using the following information. The location of the York factory is to the west of York at Upper Poppleton, just north of the A59. The location of Better Bake Ltd is between the museum and historic house, next to the A58 in Halifax.

(c) What is the straight line distance between the two factories?

(d) (i) Study the map carefully and suggest what transport systems might be used to deliver the 20 tonne load.
(ii) For each transport system, write a list of advantages and disadvantages that each might have.

Ed Badley does not favour the rail route, chiefly because Better Bake Ltd has no unloading facilities, but also because of time lost with rail wagons being shunted and standing in sidings. For these reasons, and in particular the ability of a road bulk tanker to respond quickly to an order from a factory, Ed prefers to use road transport.

Activity 7:4

(a) Use tracing paper and a pencil to trace what you consider to be the best route for a 20 tonne bulk delivery tanker from the York factory to Better Bake Ltd. Remember that the size of the vehicle shown in Figure 7.7 limits your choice to motorways, dual carriageways, A and B roads.

(b) Compare your route with three chosen by Ed Badley, which are shown in Figure 7.9. Mark them carefully on your tracing, using different colours to show: motorways, dual carriageways, A and B roads, urban A and B roads (those that pass through built-up areas).

(c) At first sight, which route looks the shortest in distance and which looks the shortest in time? State which one you would recommend and give reasons for your choice.

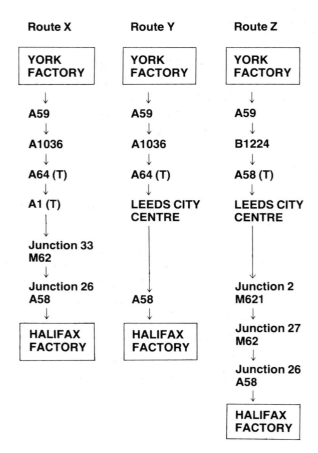

Route X	Route Y	Route Z
YORK FACTORY	YORK FACTORY	YORK FACTORY
↓	↓	↓
A59	A59	A59
↓	↓	↓
A1036	A1036	B1224
↓	↓	↓
A64 (T)	A64 (T)	A58 (T)
↓	↓	↓
A1 (T)	LEEDS CITY CENTRE	LEEDS CITY CENTRE
↓		
Junction 33 M62		
↓	↓	↓
Junction 26 A58	A58	Junction 2 M621
↓	↓	↓
HALIFAX FACTORY	HALIFAX FACTORY	Junction 27 M62
		↓
		Junction 26 A58
		↓
		HALIFAX FACTORY

▲ Figure 7.9   Routes chosen by Ed Badley
(*Note*: the short section of motorway in Leeds city centre, which has seven junctions with limited interchange, is to be considered as an urban A road)

Evaluation

A professional transport planner like Ed Badley cannot base his decision just on what looks like a good route. He has to work out exactly what is involved in each route in terms of distance, time and cost.

Activity 7:5

To work out the exact distance, you first need to copy the chart shown in Table 7.2. Then measure the distance, in kilometres, on Map 8 of each particular road type, on each route. Enter the distances on your chart. Which is the shortest route in terms of distance in kilometres?

Activity 7:6

To work out the time taken on each type of road, use the running speeds and formula shown in Table 7.3. For each route, enter the appropriate figures in the remaining spaces in your copy of Table 7.2. Which is the shortest route in terms of time?

Table 7.2   Route Evaluation Chart: distance and time

	Motorway	Dual carriageway	A and B roads	Urban A & B roads	TOTAL
Your best route: distance (km) time (min)					
Route X: distance (km) time (min)					
Route Y: distance (km) time (min)					
Route Z: distance (km) time (min)					

Table 7.3 Running speeds and formula

Road type	Average speed
Motorway	72 kph (45 mph)
Dual carriageway	56 kph (35 mph)
A and B roads	40 kph (25 mph)
Urban A and B Roads	24 kph (15 mph)

$$\text{time taken} = \frac{\text{distance along road type}}{\text{average speed for road type}} \times 60 \text{ minutes}$$

Activity 7:7

To help work out the cost of each route, copy Table 7.4. Now consider the two sorts of cost involved.

Standing costs are £12 per hour or 20 pence per minute, just to own a bulk tanker lorry. This is the cost of the vehicle in the first place, about £35 000, plus the cost of motor tax, £900 per year, the drivers' wages, and so on. Calculating standing costs for each route means you have to multiply the total number of minutes for each journey by 20 pence.

Running costs to pay for diesel fuel, tyres, maintenance, etc, are 22 pence per kilometre. To calculate these costs, multiply the total number of kilometres by 22 pence.

Enter the calculations for both sorts of costs on your copy of Table 7.4. Add the standing and running costs together to find the cheapest route.

Table 7.4 Route evaluation chart: cost

	Standing cost + running cost = total costs		
Your best route	+	=	
Route X	+	=	
Route Y	+	=	
Route Z	+	=	

Activity 7:8

Write a brief report titled 'British Sugar Corporation Route Evaluation: York to Halifax'. Explain, giving reasons, which route you would choose. Apart from distance, time and cost, try to think of other reasons to back up your choice.

Activity 7:9

Route planning has to take into account the unexpected.

(a) Suggest an alternative route if the local radio tells you there is dense fog covering all the land south of Tadcaster and east of Leeds city centre. Draw your route in the same manner as the flow diagram used in Figure 7.9.

(b) If a road accident blocked Route X, where would be the most inconvenient place for it to happen? Give two reasons to support your answer.

Activity 7:10

(a) Suppose there was money available to build a 20 kilometre stretch of motorway somewhere in the region shown on the map. Where would you prefer it to be built to ease the distribution of sugar over the whole region?

(b) How does the route planning that you have just done differ from the planning needed for:
(i) a company running coach tours;
(ii) a bus company;
(iii) a family planning a day out in the countryside in a private car?

CHAPTER 8

Wildscape

What can you learn from this chapter?

It can:
1 Show you one of Britain's wildscapes
2 Let you use map skills to locate a person in the wilderness
3 Allow you to devise ways of rescuing this person

A wildscape?

'The wind seems to blow constantly through the jagged, frost-shattered precipices. Angular rocks are strewn everywhere. Here and there lie pockets of snow. Some persist throughout the year, for the average yearly temperature hovers around freezing point. A thick snowfall in the cold, harsh winter is matched by heavy rain in the short, cool summer. Vegetation is sparse: just a few hardy plants, clinging tenaciously to life'.

Does this place sound like a wildscape? Where could it be? Alaska? Siberia? In fact, it is in Britain. It is a description of conditions at the top of Ben Nevis, Britain's highest mountain at 1344 metres. You can see it in the middle of Figure 8.1. As you might imagine, the view from the top of this mountain can be magnificent, extending in all directions for anything up to one hundred and fifty miles in clear conditions.

The summit can be reached by walkers, taking the relatively gentle zig-zagging route, which you can see in Figure 8.1. Ben Nevis, however, also offers a challenge to those hardy members of our society, the climbers, who prefer the more difficult route up the craggy north-east side of the mountain. This face is the largest crag in Britain, with many difficult climbs.

Despite the popularity of Ben Nevis, it is still dominated more by nature than by people and, therefore, it qualifies as a wildscape. The mountain is also shown on Map 9 (page 100), which is an O.S. 1:25 000 map. Symbols for it can be found on Key 3 on page 36.

Activity 8:1

(a) The photographer for Figure 8.1 viewed Ben Nevis from the west north west. Work with a partner and use two books to orient the map to match the photograph. Find the following features on the photograph: Glen Nevis; the valley containing Allt a Mhuilinn; the hill, Meall an t-Suidhe; the gully from this hill called Slochd an Daimh; the Youth Hostel (notice the gully is in a line with it).

(b) An aerial photograph like Figure 8.1 usually contains some DEAD GROUND, that is, land hidden from view. Find out where, on the photograph, the following features are hidden: the loch called Lochan Meall an t-Suidhe; Carn Mor Dearg Arête; the Charles Inglis Clark (CIC) hut; Nevis Forest.

(c) Estimate the time of year and time of day when the photograph was taken.

Lost and injured

James MacIntosh put down his soup spoon.
'I thought I heard a knock at the door,' he said to
his wife. 'Somebody wants a bed, no doubt.'
He rose and went to the door of the Youth Hostel
and opened it to find Simon Murphy leaning on
the door post, looking wet and exhausted. He
was wearing a waterproof jacket, jeans and
walking boots and he looked all in.
'Can you help me please?' he asked urgently.
'My mate's hurt and still up on the mountain.'

James quickly extracted the rest of Simon's
story. It seems that Simon and his friend, Peter
Nicholson, were from Liverpool and were on
holiday in Scotland. While staying at Fort William
on the previous night, they had decided to climb
Ben Nevis. The landlady of the guest house had
pointed to the high clouds just obscuring the sun
and had warned them that the weather might turn
bad, but they had ignored her advice. They had
left their car not far from the Youth Hostel.

Both boys were nineteen and had walked a
little on the hills in North Wales when they were at

school, so they knew that they should take
waterproof jackets. They both wore jeans and
Peter wore training shoes; boots always felt too
heavy for him, he had said. They took a lunch and
some spare pullovers in a knapsack and they
had followed the path over the footbridge across
the River Nevis at the Youth Hostel at about 8.30
that morning.

Both lads played amateur soccer back in
Liverpool, so they were reasonably fit, though the
path was steep and tiring. After passing near a
loch they found that the most difficult part was
where the path zig-zagged from side to side
across a scree slope. Then, just as the path
began to get easier, and they could sense that
the top of the mountain was not far away, the
cloud lowered and the mountain was covered in
mist. Simon was all for going back – after all, they
hadn't brought a map or a compass – but Peter
wanted to get to the top. They continued and,
having reached the top, they ate some of their
lunch and started their return journey. As the
drizzle turned to rain, they decided to avoid the
zig-zagging path and take a short cut, a
straighter path across the scree. They jumped
over a stream and soon realised they had lost the
path. They could see only a few metres in the fog

▼ Figure 8.1   Aerial photograph of Ben Nevis

Table 8.1 The effect of surface type on search time

(relates to optional rule (e)). N.B. More difficult surfaces add more time to a search.

Symbol	Surface type	Extra search time
(rough grassland symbol)	Rough grassland	none
(grassland and boulders symbol)	Rough grassland and boulders	¼ hour
(grassland and scree symbol)	Rough grassland and scree	½ hour
(scree symbol)	Scree	¾ hour
(loose rock symbol)	Loose rock	¾ hour
(woodland symbol)	Woodland	¾ hour
(rock outcrops symbol)	Rock outcrops	1 hour
(rock outcrops and scree symbol)	Rock outcrops and scree or boulders	1½ hours

and they thought that, by walking across the scree slope without going down, they might find the loch. They seemed to have walked for ages, once slipping into a stream, but they struggled on.

They left the scree behind, but did not find the loch. They lost track of time for neither of them wore a watch. What followed became a nightmare as they began to panic. They stumbled this way and that, finding and then losing the path, jumping streams and tripping over boulders. Then disaster struck! Peter slipped on a wet boulder and hurt his leg badly. He couldn't walk and he was in a lot of pain.

Calling for help was no use. The fog and the rain seemed to swallow their cries. Simon decided to go for help, leaving Peter the food and spare clothes.

Simon remembers only a few things from the next two hours. He climbed up and down, crossed streams, jumped over a wall, passed a line of posts, climbed a hill slipping on rocky outcrops and finally slid and scrambled down a steep hillside, before he reached a path he recognised, which led him, finally, back to the Youth Hostel. The only things that he could remember about the place where he had left Peter were that it was grassy and scattered with boulders and there was the sound of a stream rushing nearby. By the time his story was complete, the Mountain Rescue Group had arrived from Fort William.

Activity 8:2

Your task is to act as controller of the Mountain Rescue Group. Your aim is to find Peter as soon as possible, because there are only five hours of daylight left. The longer he stays on the mountain, the less likely he is to survive.

The weather is very poor, visibility is down to ten metres. Your Mountain Rescue Group works in four teams of ten people each, and a single team can search one quarter of a square kilometre in one hour.

As controller of the four teams, use the method of searching explained in (a) to (d).

(a) Place tracing paper over the map, marking the corners of the map on the tracing paper. Trace, with a solid line, the route taken by Peter and Simon as far as you are sure of it. Trace, with a dashed line, any parts of the route of which you are less sure. Include Simon's final journey to the Youth Hostel.

(b) Study Simon's account of the day again and list any clues that may help you discover Peter's whereabouts.

(c) Carefully choose four quarter-squares to be searched by your four teams, A, B, C and D, from anywhere on the map. Outline them on your tracing paper and mark them A1, B1, C1 and D1.

(d) Work out the time taken by each of your search teams. This may include extra time added if your teacher wants you to use the optional rules

Figure 8.2 Controller's time chart

First search attempt

Search team	Time taken to search first quarter-square	Extra time added by optional rules			Total time taken by each team	Check with teacher: Peter found √ Peter not found ×
		(e)	(f)	(g)		
A						
B						
C						
D						

Second search attempt

Search team	Total time taken after first search attempt	Time taken to search second quarter-square	Extra time added by optional rules			Total time taken by each team	Check with teacher: Peter found √ Peter not found ×
			(e)	(f)	(g)		
A							
B							
C							
D							

Third search attempt

Search team	Total time taken after second search attempt	Time taken to search third quarter-square	Extra time added by optional rules			Total time taken by each team	Check with teacher: Peter found √ Peter not found ×
			(e)	(f)	(g)		
A							
B							
C							
D							

Fourth search attempt

Search team	Total time taken after third search attempt	Time taken to search fourth quarter-square	Extra time added by optional rules			Total time taken by each team	Check with teacher: Peter found √ Peter not found ×
			(e)	(f)	(g)		
A							
B							
C							
D							

Fifth search attempt

Search team	Total time taken after fourth search attempt	Time taken to search fifth quarter-square	Extra time added by optional rules			Total time taken by each team	Check with teacher: Peter found √ Peter not found ×
			(e)	(f)	(g)		
A							
B							
C							
D							

Table 8.2   The effect of slope angles on search time
(relates to optional rule (f))

N.B. Steeper slopes add more time to a search.

Number of contours visible in hole	Slope angle (in degrees)	Extra search time (in hours)
0–1	less than 3	none
2–4	4–15	¼
5–7	16–25	½
8–10	26–34	1
11–13	35–41	1½
14 or more	more than 42°	too dangerous to climb in this weather – abandon search in this square

Slope angles are calculated by considering that the horizontal distance on the ground, across a 6 mm hole held over a map, is 150 metres. Vertical distance is shown roughly by the number of contours. Slope angle equals the tangent of vertical over horizontal distances.

(e) to (h). Enter these times on a copy of Figure 8.2 and check with your teacher to see if one of your groups has found Peter. If they have, your teacher will give you his exact location and you can go on to Activity 8:3. If not, then have a second attempt at searching, choosing four more quarter-squares and marking them A2, B2, C2, and D2 on your tracing paper. Then work through (d) again. If you have not found Peter after four attempts, question your teacher, who will play the part of Simon Murphy, to see if you can extract any more clues to Peter's whereabouts.

(e) This *optional rule* introduces *the effect of the type of surface* on the time taken for searching. Decide which of the surface types shown in Table 8.1 covers the largest part of each chosen quarter-square. Add the extra search time involved to your copy of Figure 8.2. Is each of your teams still within the five hours available to them?

(f) This *optional rule* introduces *the effect of slope angles* on search times. Place the six millimetre hole made by a standard paper punch over the centre of the quarter-square that you want to search. Count the number of contours you can see through this hole and find that number in Table 8.2. Notice the slope angle and write the extra time on to Figure 8.2. Again, remember that only five hours, in total, are available to each search team.

(g) This *optional rule* shows how *time spent walking* to and from the chosen quarter-squares can add extra time to the search. Remember each of your four search teams walks from the Youth Hostel to their first quarter-square. If Peter is not found at the first attempt, add the time taken to reach the quarter-squares of the second attempt. There is no extra time if the search team's quarter-squares touch each other.

To work out walking time, measure the horizontal distance along a route to or between quarter-squares and estimate one hour for every four kilometres (i.e. 100 metres = 1.5 minutes). Now work out the vertical distances climbed and estimate one hour for every six hundred metres up, but not downwards (i.e. 100 metres up = 10 minutes). Add both figures together.

As an example, the time taken for one team to walk from the Youth Hostel at 127 717 to the beginning of the line of posts marking a Mountain Rescue Route at 146 724 would be about 1 hour 40 minutes. This is because horizontal distance along the path is 2.75 km, i.e. 40 minutes. Vertical distance is 580 metres, i.e. just under 60 minutes. Hence, approximately 1 hour 40 minutes in total.

(h) This *optional rule* allows the confident controller to call out *fewer search teams* and therefore reduce the overall search time. This will mean less time and money wasted for all. The most successful controller will locate the injured walker in the quickest time and with the fewest people.

If you think you can locate Peter with only one, two or three teams, then do so. You may call out more for later attempts if your hunch was wrong and you did not find him.

Rescue and report

Peter, the injured hill walker, has been on the mountain for a whole day. For much of the day he has been badly injured, soaked to the skin and exhausted. It is quite likely that he is suffering from HYPOTHERMIA, a dangerous condition when the body temperature becomes drastically lowered. He needs hospital treatment immediately and an ambulance is waiting at the Youth Hostel.

Activity 8:3

Plan a helicopter rescue. By the time your search group has located Peter and strapped him to a stretcher, the cloud base has lifted to six hundred metres above sea level.

The nearest R.A.F. helicopter base is to the south. Plan a route for the pilot, writing your instructions in the form of a concise radio message. The helicopter will fly into the map area above grid reference 137 701. The pilot needs to know precise distances, directions, points and heights to fly at.

Activity 8:4

(a) Your job as controller of the Mountain Rescue Group involves writing an official report about a rescue incident. It must be written so that it will not be misinterpreted. You must, therefore, avoid critical comment and concern yourself only with the facts. To help you write the report, consider the hints on Mountain Safety, described in Figure 8.3.

(b) Local newspaper reporters do not need to stick to facts alone. They want to make the report interesting to their readers. Act as a reporter and write a brief report for the local Fort William newspaper. Write a headline to catch the eye and a report to interest local people.

Mountain Safety

Clothing   Let it be warm, with a windproof anorak and waterproof outer covering (cagoule) plus trousers. Have headgear – balaclava, hood. Carry woollen gloves. Don't wear shorts or jeans; they give absolutely no protection when wet. Carry one or two spare jerseys.

Footgear   Wear boots rather than shoes. Nailed soles are best for the wet slippery conditions usually found in Great Britain. Vibram type are the next best, preferably with the addition of a few nails. Boots which have a sloping front edge to the heel should be avoided: they slip easily on wet grass. Smooth soles should never be worn on the hills.

Food   Always carry some extra food for emergency, e.g. sweets, chocolate, glucose tablets.

Maps and compass   Always carry the relevant map with you, preferably Ordnance Survey, but, first, know how to read and use it properly. Carry it on your person, not in your rucksack. This goes for the compass, too. Learn and know how to use the Grid Reference system. A magnifying glass is a refinement, but can be very helpful at times.

Whistle and torch   Carry a whistle and torch for signalling.

Watch   Carry a watch: check every so often that it hasn't stopped.

Emergency shelter   Carry a survival bag or tent for shelter

Messages   In an emergency, messages will have to be written. You must therefore have pencil and paper.

Spectacles   If you need spectacles, you are in a bit of a spot if yours are lost or broken. Carry a spare pair.

First Aid   Carry a first aid kit with you; elastoplast, antiseptic ointment, crepe bandage for a sprain, are all useful items.

Rope   A very useful piece of special equipment for the leader of the party is a 30 or 40 foot length of light line.

Route   Give details of your route, destination and expected time of arrival to a responsible person. Let him/her know when you have arrived. If you have to make any change let him/her know as soon as possible and well before he/she gets around to calling the police.

Weather   Take note of forecasts and local information Notice Boards; if necessary, re-plan your expedition.

Getting lost   Don't! Check your position on the map frequently and especially at the moment of climbing into mist. Look back occasionally and take note of landmarks.
   Establish your walking speed by setting a target a known distance off and seeing how long it takes you to get there.
   Observe the time of day by your watch frequently.

If you do get lost   Don't panic! Establish where you believe you are, from your last known position, and decide on the compass direction you need to take.
   Trust your compass absolutely.
   Streams can be good guides downhill, but they often fall over precipices, so be cautious of them.

Obviously, it is dangerous to walk alone: a group of 4 or more is desirable.

For extra information consult *Mountain and Cave Rescue*, Handbook of the Mountain Rescue Committee. Available from: The Secretary, Mountain Rescue Committee, 9 Milldale Avenue, Temple Meads, Buxton, Derbyshire, SK17 9BE.

▲ Figure 8.3   Mountain safety

As you have seen, wildscape areas can pose special problems for people. The hazardous nature of such areas, however, varies greatly with the time of year, the weather, the fitness and experience of people who venture into them. How can we reduce accidents in wildscapes? Should we restrict the movement of people in such areas? Are we overprotecting the majority for the sake of the foolish minority? The following activity considers these important questions.

Activity 8:5

(a) If you were asked to advise how to improve safety and reduce accidents on mountains like Ben Nevis, what suggestions would you make?

(b) What signs are there on Map 9 that mountain safety on Ben Nevis is considered important? How do you think each of these features might be used?

(c) If money became available for another small shelter to be built on the mountain, where would you build it and why?

(d) If you had to zone the mountain into areas to be avoided by the general public, which areas do you consider high risk and why?

(e) To what extent should official bodies like the police, local councils and National Park authorities influence what an individual does in a wildscape?

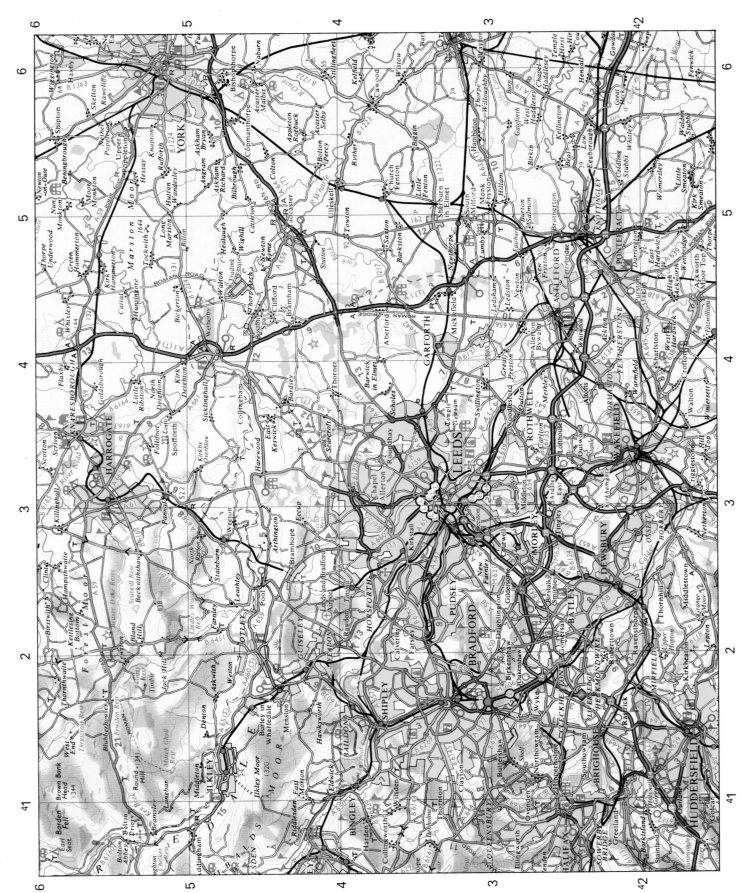

Map 8

Map 8 York and the West Riding (1:250 000)

Map 9

Map 9 Ben Nevis (1:25 000)

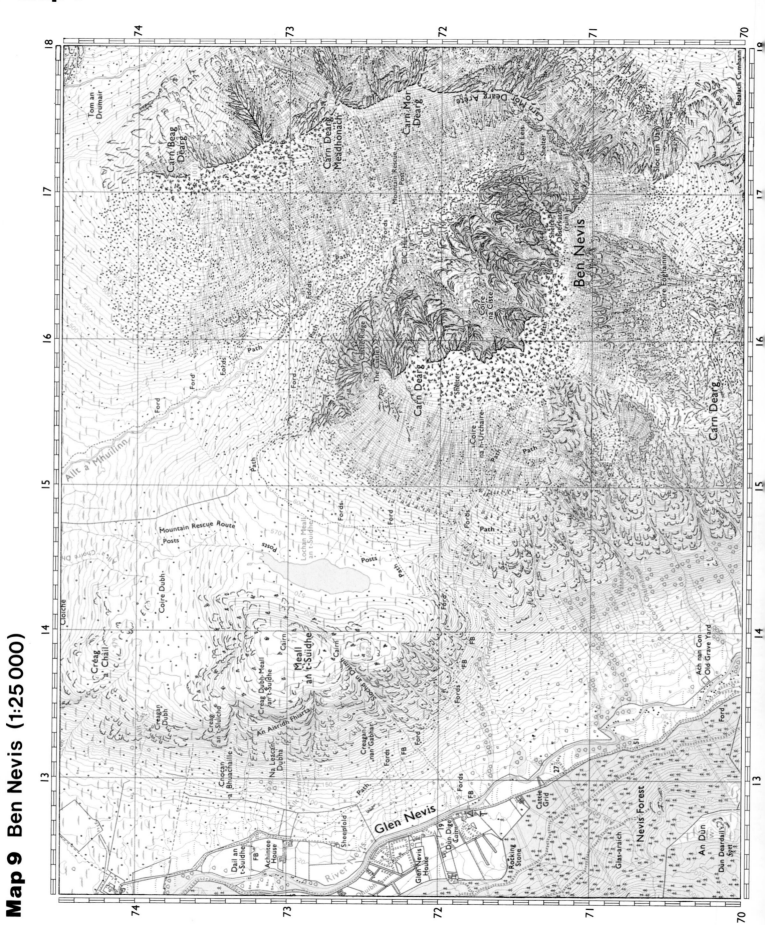

CHAPTER 9

Cityscape

What can you learn from this chapter?

It can:

1 Show you some of the problems of inner city landscapes
2 Let you plan possible solutions to these problems in one such area
3 Help you judge your plan against the feelings of the local people
4 Allow you to find further solutions in the outer city landscape

Figure 9.1 Oblique aerial photograph of inner city Coventry

Inner city landscapes

There are nearly four million people living in Britain's inner cities and even more who work or do their shopping there. Figure 9.1 shows the layout of Coventry's inner city area. The complicated mixture of land uses and buildings that you can see in the photograph is typical of inner city areas throughout the country.

Activity 9:1

Points A to F on Figure 9.1 show a variety of land uses. Look at the area surrounding each point carefully and describe what you see around points A to E. Refer to the way the land might be used, the type of buildings and their quality. As an example, point F might be described as follows:

'The land around point F has high and low rise flats, separated by patches of grass and roads. They are newly built and in good condition. A new building is being added between the main road and the flats.'

What features did you pick out at point A? Did you spot that these buildings are mainly large shops and offices? In fact, this area is the central business district (CBD) of Coventry. It is very different from the landscape nearby. The land outside the ring road (easily spotted because, as its name suggests, it forms a ring around the CBD) has older factories and terraced houses on it. They stand side by side with patches of derelict land or car parks. There are also some newer blocks of flats like those at point F.

One such place, lying just outside the CBD, is the Eagle Street area. You can find it on Figure 9.1 at point G. Figure 9.2 shows what it looks like when viewed from directly above.

▼ Figure 9.2   Vertical aerial photograph of the Eagle Street area

Activity 9:2

(a) Can you spot any features that appear on both photographs? If so, suggest which land uses are represented by these features.

(b) You may find the viewpoint of Figure 9.2 a little unusual, though it is more like a map than Figure 9.1. It is still possible to recognise land uses on it. List those that you can identify in addition to those noted in (a).

(c) Compare Figure 9.1 and 9.2. Briefly suggest advantages and disadvantages of both types of photograph for:
(i) finding your way around a city you know quite well;
(ii) planning the route of a new urban motorway.

(d) Figures 9.3, 9.4 and 9.5 show the kind of glimpses you might have of an area similar to the Eagle Street area if you drove through it.
(i) What would be your immediate reactions to the place? Think of words to describe your feelings.
(ii) Think about your reactions. Why did you react in this way?
(iii) Compare your reactions with those of other people in your class.

(e) Study Map 10 on pages 104–5, which is an O.S. 1:1250 map of the Eagle Street area. Compare it with Figure 9.2.
(i) What can you spot on the photograph that is not marked on the map?
(ii) What information is marked on the map but not found on the photograph?
(iii) The O.S. map, Map 10, has the largest scale of all current O.S. maps. To gain an idea of this scale, copy a stretch of Foleshill Road from the map onto your own paper, keeping the same scale. Then add to your drawing the plan of a double-decker bus, which is eleven metres long by two and a half metres wide. Remember to use the same scale for your plan of the bus. The 1:1250 scale can be found in Key 1 on page 17.

Figure 9.3 (top)   Inner city derelict land
Figure 9.4 (centre)   Inner city housing
Figure 9.5 (bottom)   Inner city industry

Map 10 Eagle Street - Coventry (1:1250)

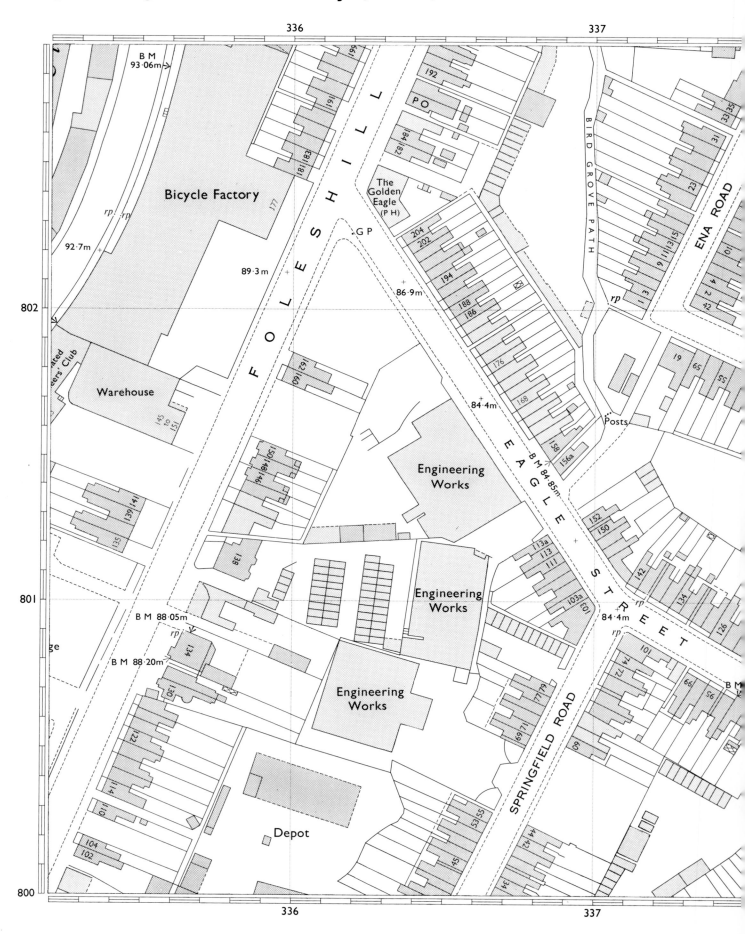

Map 10

338

339

340

THORNHILL ROAD

89

76

84

44

36

28

20

12

4 2

31

15 13 11

3 1

28

20

12

4 2

...LAND ROAD

31

23

15 13 11

3 1

...orks

Sub Sta

67 69

75 77

P

rp

90·2m

92

96

86

131

121

119

115

113

111

107

105

Hall

90·2m

BM 90·78m
90·2m

159

151

143

141

128

132 134

120

118

183

175

167

BM 91·35m

90·5m

150

142 140

LEICESTER CAUSEWAY

rp

John Gulson
Primary School

802

PCB

801

69

64

59

198

74

Mosque

55 67

85 87

77

98

82

74

66

64

64b

62a

GEORGE STREET

Eagle House

7 9
12

9 6

24 22

11

8 6

113

87·5m

89·6m

rp

rp

84 82
56 58

76

68

60 58

EAGLE

87·8m

rp

STREET

Spiritualists'
National
Church

57

55 57

47

39 37

55

27 29

5 9
3 0

54

Garage

47

47

89

35 37

Meth
Church

800

338

339

340

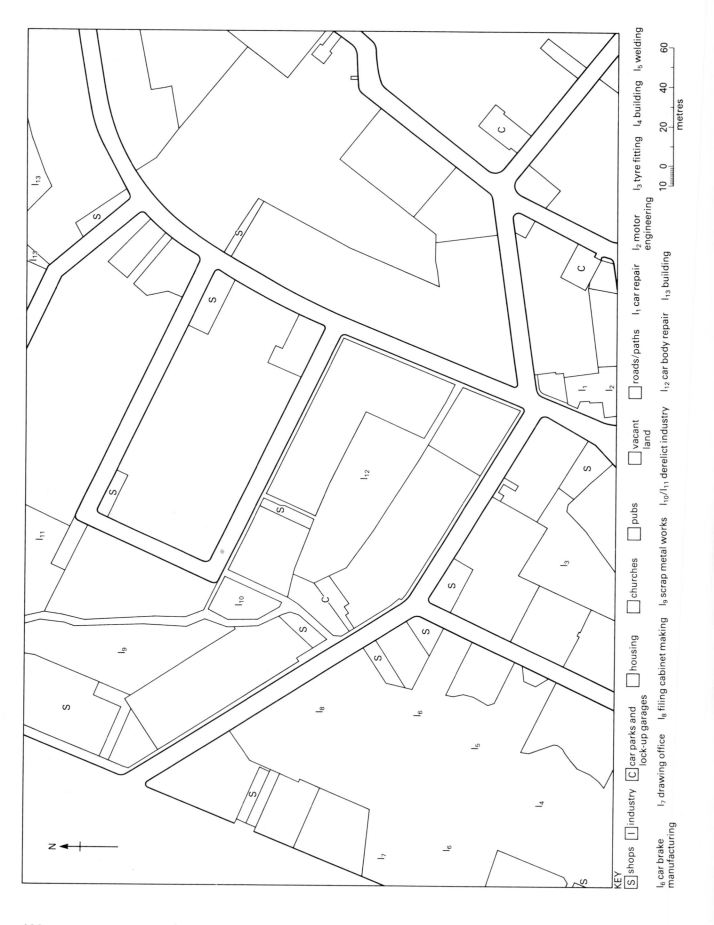

KEY

S shops I industry C car parks and lock-up garages housing churches pubs vacant land roads/paths

I_1 car repair I_2 motor engineering I_3 tyre fitting I_4 building I_5 welding

I_6 car brake manufacturing I_7 drawing office I_8 filing cabinet making I_9 scrap metal works I_{10}/I_{11} derelict industry I_{12} car body repair I_{13} building

N

10 0 20 40 60
metres

Activity 9:3

Your main task in this chapter will be to present a planner's solution to the problems that face the Eagle Street area. Naturally, this means studying the area carefully to find the problems that exist there.

(a) On a copy of Figure 9.6, use colours to shade in the land uses of the Eagle Street area. Industrial areas, shops and car parks have been indicated. You have to decide the use of each remaining patch by studying Figure 9.2 and Map 10. Note that land West of Foleshill Road lies out of the study area.

(b) In a sentence, try to describe the pattern of land use shown on your completed copy of Figure 9.6.

Activity 9:4

The completed LAND USE MAP forms a useful starting point for examining some of the problems and conflicts that the area might have.

(a) Local people may have differing feelings about: the motor body repair works, which is industry I12 on the map, the hall in Newland Road, which is used for weekend discos; the Spiritualists' National Church in Eagle Street.
  Explain how you think the opinions of the following people may differ:
(i) Geoff Morgan, 51, landlord of the Golden Eagle, whose son is an apprentice at industry I12;
(ii) Jane Stevens, 83, resident at 33, Newland Road for forty-five years and still regularly attends the Methodist church;
(iii) Ranjit Singh, 38, who came from India in 1965 and now runs the newsagent / tobacconist shop at 47, Leicester Causeway.

(b) Invent names, addresses and backgrounds for further residents, factory workers or factory owners in the area and suggest how they might feel about: the heavy traffic on Foleshill Road; the primary school; the row of derelict buildings 65–87 (odd numbers only) George Street.

◀ Figure 9.6   Outline land use map of the Eagle Street area

(c) What would your own feelings be about the six land uses in (a) and (b) if they were in:
(i)   your home street;
(ii) your neighbourhood;
(iii) someone else's neighbourhood?

(d) How would you react if plans existed for:
(i) rerouting heavy traffic along your nearest road;
(ii) building an indoor swimming pool either next door to your house or half a mile away;
(iii) opening a fish and chip shop either next door or half a mile away?
Give reasons for your reactions.

From the work you have completed so far, you may have been able to see some of the more obvious problems of the area. It is necessary, however, to look even more closely at it to discover *all* the problems. You need this information before you can begin to plan any changes. To help you further, Figure 9.7 shows a summary of information which was gathered in a survey of the Eagle Street area. Five items in the survey are shown in the graphs in Figure 9.8.

Activity 9:5

(a) Use the information shown by the graphs in Figure 9.8 to complete the five spaces left on your copy of Figure 9.7. To do this, you need to make up one short sentence describing the most important feature(s) of the Eagle Street graphs in comparison with the graphs of Coventry as a whole.

(b) Perhaps the overall picture may appear depressing, but there are many positive features. On your copy of Figure 9.7, underline, using two different colours, the features of the area that local people might consider to be positive or negative.

(c) It is possible to take two contrasting viewpoints of life in the Eagle Street area. Pretend that you live there and, using the information you have met so far:
(i) try to compose a poem or song to a tune you already know, as a protest against the environment of Eagle Street; or
(ii) write a letter to your old home in India, trying to persuade your elderly parents to come and live with you.

HOUSING
- Terraced houses built before 1914
- Most have minimum future life of at least 10 years
- Very poor or derelict buildings – 35/37, 47–59 (odd), 48–62 (odd), 65–87 (odd) George Street
  1–29 (odd), 37–52 (odd), 58–62 (even), Eagle Street
  114–118 (even), 124, 146–150 (even), 160 Foleshill Road
  143–149 (odd), 183 Leicester Causeway
- All lack running hot water, inside toilets and baths
- Housing is in demand especially for the larger family

INCOME AND EMPLOYMENT
- Incomes below average, high unemployment
- 25% work locally
- Large numbers work in the hospital, catering, public transport, office cleaning
- 25% walk to work
- Many students
- Car ownership . . . .
. . . .
. . . .
. . . .
- Occupation type . . . .
. . . .
. . . .
. . . .

RECREATION
- Places and equipment for children almost non-existent

INDUSTRY
- Long established
- Cramped, awkwardly shaped sites
- Expansion is therefore limited
- Businesses are small but important employers
- They rely on local people and local trade
- Does not fit together well with neighbouring land uses

SCHOOL
- Recently rebuilt
- Needs more playing fields
- Only just enough pupils from local area

SHOPS
- City centre shops within one kilometre
- 50% shop there at least weekly
- 40% use local shops daily
- Local shops supply convenience goods such as bread, groceries, etc.
- Local shops supply goods like Asian foods not available elsewhere
- Local shops open for long hours

ENVIRONMENT
- Low quality
- Few trees, little grass
- Few footpaths away from road
- Heavy traffic on Foleshill Road

RESIDENCE
- 25% lived in area for over 20 years
- 25% lived in area for under 2 years
- Tenure . . . .
. . . .
- Household size . . . .
. . . .

SOCIAL FACILITIES
- Few in number
- Pubs and churches are important to different parts of community

PEOPLE
- Birthplaces . . . .
. . . .
. . . .
. . . .
- Close knit social contacts
- 30% of families have relatives locally
- 30% of families have close friends nearby
- 40% of families belong to voluntary groups like churches and the mosque

ASIAN COMMUNITY
- Close-knit
- Family and friend relationships important
- Lives often centred on churches and mosques
- Small Asian corner shops important in community
- Prefer to own houses if possible
- Low desire for car ownership
- 40% of heads of foreign households have difficulty speaking English.

▲ Figure 9.7   Results of physical and social survey in the Eagle Street area

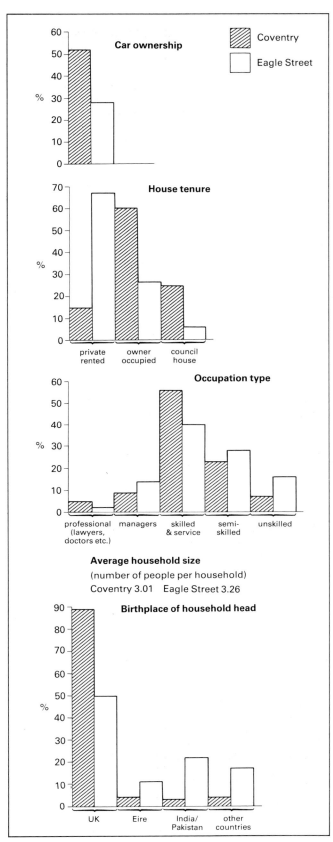

▲ Figure 9.8 Statistics about people in Eagle Street, compared with Coventry as a whole

Town planning teams

The West Midlands County Council had to choose areas that had an urgent need for change. The land east of Foleshill Road was chosen, for the reasons you have now considered, and called the Eagle Street Action Area. This means that money is available to completely rebuild, partly rebuild or simply improve the area. What should be done? This difficult job, of planning the future use of Eagle Street, is given to the town planners.

Activity 9:6

(a) Your job is to work in a team of town planners to plan the future land use of the Eagle Street Action Area. Your aim is to produce a map, showing how you think the land should be used in the future, and to write a brief report to justify your decisions.

You will be given a role to play in a town planning team by your teacher. Details of each role are set out below. They tell you of the problems that each planner must consider and you have to work out ways to solve them.

Advice

1 Be imaginative. Have you made the *best* use of a particular piece of land? Could you make a better use of it by combining a number of land uses?

2 Be prepared to 'give-and-take'. What happens if your ideas clash with someone else's? You may need to compromise.

3 Be aware of priorities. Which land uses are most important? Which are least important? You may not be able to solve *all* the problems.

4 Be mindful of time. How might your ideas work in six months, two years or ten years time?

5 Lastly, remember that you are dealing with people! If it helps, imagine that you live in one of the houses on the map. Would you be happy to live in the environment you have planned?

(i) *The Housing Planner* must consider the problems of providing housing for people and suggest ways of: increasing the number of houses; improving their quality; finding a site for twelve old people's flats. The flats will cover a site approximately the size of the hall in Newland Road.

(ii) *The Industry Planner* must consider the problems of providing work for people and suggest ways of: keeping existing industry to make work for local people; finding more land to allow industries to grow; trying to move industry from cramped sites and away from areas of land use with which they might clash.

(iii) *The Recreation and Education Planner* must consider the problems of recreation and suggest ways of: providing several small (say 10 × 10 metre), safe play spaces for toddlers and pre-school children; providing two larger (say 30 × 30 metre) play spaces for five- to nine-year-olds; providing one 'kickabout' area for older juniors and younger teenagers, and; providing a larger area (at least one hectare, i.e. 100 metres × 100 metres) for school playing fields.

(iv) *The Environment Planner* must consider the general environmental quality and suggest ways of reducing eyesores; find suitable patches of ground to be planted with trees, shrubs and grass; find places where screens of trees may be planted to reduce noise or unpleasant views.

(b) When you have drawn a land-use map to show your ideas, and written the report, prepare a short talk to explain your ideas to the rest of the class. As a planning team, try to explain *how* you reached your decisions, including, for example, any compromises you made. Try to judge your own plan. What are its strengths and weaknesses?

That's my home

So far your work in this chapter has been following a path similar to the work actually done by the planners. You have *identified the problems*, *surveyed the area*, been given certain *objectives* and produced a *design*. The next stage is *evaluation* and it is here that public opinion is important. The last stage is *implementation* (i.e. producing the final plan and actually doing what the plan suggests). The decision is made by the politicians, not the planners.

Geoff Dowson (55) is owner of the motor body repair works (Industry I12). He would not want his firm moved. He has just spent a lot of money improving the equipment and much of his trade comes from the local area.

Liz Platt (50) is headmistress of the John Gulson Primary School. She says, 'We have to take our children by bus to the nearest playing field to play games. The situation has become very difficult and we must have more land.'

June Baird (48) is Managing Director of the filing cabinet makers (I8). She would like to expand her works, employing ten new workers. This may double the existing area of the factory.

Imrhat Patel (67) is an Indian who has retired from his job as caretaker of the Hall in Newland Road. He lives in a run-down rented house at 45 Eagle Street. He would dearly like a small, modern flat, preferably as close as possible to his son's home at 89 Eagle Street.

Peter Hughes (13) and **Latif Matander** (14) are two local lads living in Thornhill Road. They are mostly interested in finding somewhere to play soccer.

Gladys Smith (58) looks after a sick husband and they live at 1 Ena Road. She says, 'We both find the noise and view of the scrapyard (I9) very unpleasant. We are also really fed up with the rubbish that is dumped on the derelict site (I10) next to our home.'

Sophie Tamsin (29) is a housewife living in the grocer's shop at 162 Foleshill Road. She and her husband have worked hard to improve it. Her biggest concerns are with the standard of schooling and for the safety of her children, aged 4, 8 and 10, as they play in the area.

Jim McNamara (18) lives at 153 Leicester Causeway. He is unemployed but he has metal-working skills.

Reverend Barry Cripps (43) is the Minister of the Methodist Church in Eagle Street. He says, 'I am particularly worried about the quality of the local housing and about the lack of jobs in the area.'

▲ Figure 9.9   Some residents, factory owners and workers in the Eagle Street area

Activity 9:7

One or two planning teams will be chosen to present their designs to the rest of the class. Those who are not planners will act the parts of the people of Eagle Street, at a 'public enquiry' in your classroom. It would help if the chosen design(s) could be seen by everyone before the enquiry. This will help each 'resident' to decide what they like or dislike about the design, and why, and also give them time to work out constructive arguments for or against it. Each member of the class will be given a role to play which can be chosen from the three shown in Activity 9:4 or from the ten shown in Figure 9.9. Alternatively, students can make up their own roles.

Outer city landscapes

In earlier activities in this chapter you may have chosen what you considered to be the best plan for the future of the Eagle Street Action Area. Did you consider what the wider effects of your choice might be?

Change in the inner city may force people to move to find homes in the outer city. Similarly, the natural growth of a city often takes place at its edge. The following activity shows how town planners not only plan the detail of small areas like Eagle Street, but also plan the future of cities at a different scale. Map 11 on page 117 is an O.S. 1:50 000 map of Coventry. It is a city which needs to spread at its edge.

Table 9.1   Value table for possible building sites around Coventry

YOUR CHOICES

How suitable are these sites for new housing?

Factors (each given values of 1–10)	Site A SW corner of 30 81	Site B SE corner of 32 84	Site C NE corner of 34 84	Site D	Site E
Nearness to A roads and motorways					
Nearness to a school					
Nearness to possible jobs					
Nearness to attractive countryside					
TOTALS					

Note that each site covers approximately a quarter of a square kilometre.

Activity 9:8

(a) In this activity, you are asked to choose a site for new housing on the edge of Coventry, using Map 11. There are five possible sites, three listed on Table 9.1 and two more to be chosen by you. When you have chosen them, you must judge how good each site is from the point of view of nearness to A roads and motorways, nearness to jobs, nearness to schools and nearness to attractive countryside. You are to give each factor, for each site, a value of 1–10 points. A high value means the site is in a good position for that particular factor. For example, if there is a school right next to the site, and you think this is an advantage for new housing, give the site a value of 8, 9 or 10. Write this value on a copy of Table 9.1, in the correct column.

Each factor needs some thought before starting. For example, is it an advantage to be right next to industrial buildings which may provide jobs? What is 'attractive countryside'? You might discuss these thoughts in class or in smaller groups.

When you have completed Table 9.1, add up the values for each site.

(b) (i) Explain which site you prefer and why.
(ii) Describe any factors not included in Table 9.1 which make the sites better or worse for a housing development.

(c) What further kinds of information would you need to make an even better choice?

(d) Describe the advantages and disadvantages of building houses at the edges of cities.

Activity 9:9

Most people in Britain live in the changing landscapes of towns and cities. Change is frequently planned by town planners and information about such changes is available to you. Try to find out about a planning issue in your home area. Write a short essay describing and explaining the plan. Include in it your opinions of the plan, and give reasons for your opinions.

CHAPTER 10

Farmscape

What can you learn from this chapter?

It can:

1   Show you the importance of farming and the effect of farmers' decisions on the British landscape
2   Encourage you to interpret a farming and forestry landscape in North Wales
3   Allow you to judge the quality of farming land from an O.S. 1:10 000 map
4   Let you make decisions about how to use that land for various sheep farming jobs

The face of Britain

Which industry covers 78 per cent of the land in Britain? Which industry's output is worth more than the output of the entire British motor vehicle industry? Which industry employs 640 000 people? The title of the chapter gives you the answer. It is the farming industry. Some people fail to recognise the importance of farming in that, for example, it produces 60 per cent of Britain's food. It also has a major effect on the British landscape. In fact, the National Farmer's Union say that:

> 'British farmers have made much of today's landscape. The face of Britain reflects the pattern of agriculture and countless generations of farmers have each contributed to it.'

Activity 10:1

(a) Suppose your class had been asked to make a three-dimensional model of a farming landscape for use in your geography lessons. List the items that would need to be made.

(b) Try to classify the items under such headings as 'Farm Buildings', 'Natural Features', 'Farm Machinery' and so on.

(c) Discuss what kinds of items were to be made and what items you would have left out.

(d) The farming landscapes created by some of the people in the class would be different from others. Why is this so?

(e) Your choices created a model landscape but, in a real farming landscape, which groups of people influence its appearance? Which group do you think is most important?

Activity 10:2

(a) Figure 10.1 shows a landscape near Ffestiniog in North Wales. What are the main uses of the land shown in the photograph?

(b) Which parts of the landscape seem to be most affected by people, and which are least affected? Give reasons.

(c) What do you think the area of land might have looked like without interference from people?

Map 12 on page 118 is an O.S. 1:10 000 map showing a landscape in North Wales where forestry and farming blend together. Although the map may look confusing at first sight, careful study will show its important features. First, its scale is nearly the same as that of Map 3. This means that one centimetre on Map 12 represents . . . what? If you are having any problems working this out, refer back to Figure 4.9, page 51.

▲ Figure 10.1   Aerial photograph of a landscape near Ffestiniog, North Wales

Second, the symbols used for both maps are nearly identical (see Key 2A, page 35). The main difference is that larger vegetation symbols are used on the 1:10 000 map. These symbols are shown on Key 2A.

Third, you can make more sense of this map by comparing it with the aerial photograph, Figure 10.1, in the following activity.

Activity 10:3

(a) From which corner of the map was the photograph taken? Which direction was the photographer facing? (Note that 'Afon' means river.)

(b) Working with a partner, orient, or set, the map and photograph. If you are unsure how to do this, check with Activity 2:14 in Chapter 2.

(c) What land use can you see on the map that you cannot easily find in the photograph?

(d) Find, on the photograph: Afon Dwyryd; A496 road; Felinrhyd Fach; the gap in the trees showing the position of the pipelines; electricity transmission lines.

Activity 10:4

(a) Figure 10.2 is a CROSS SECTION of the valley of the Afon Prysor. Place a straight edge across the map along the line of the cross section between 665 400 and 654 390.

(b) Match the following labels to the arrows lettered A to E: very steep-sided gorge of the Afon Prysor; gently rounded hill top; steep slope facing south-west; gently sloping river terrace (a piece of nearly level land next to a river, but raised above it); steep slope facing north east.

(c) Match the following labels to the arrows numbered 1–8: airshaft for buried pipeline; path; fenced road; farm buildings; deciduous wood; sheep folds (small pens about 15 metres square, used for gathering a sheep flock together at certain times of the year); electricity transmission lines on poles; electricity transmission lines on pylons.

A youth club camp

Felinrhyd Fach is a farm belonging to Mr and Mrs Alun Williams and their land is shown in Map 12, marked as sections A to G. As you may have found, maps can come to life with the help of your imagination and by an appreciation of such things as scale, distance and symbols. To help you with the following activity, use the symbols and scale shown in Key 2A.

Mr Williams has received a letter from Stuart Lindeman, a youth club leader in Birmingham. Stuart wants to hire a patch of land for a month-long summer camp in August. He has a large party of fourteen-year-old boys and girls and he needs about 0.25 hectare (50 × 50 metres or 2500 square metres) of land. Mr. Williams has written the letter shown in Figure 10.3, in reply to Stuart.

Activity 10:5

(a) Stuart cannot visit the farm before August, so he has decided to choose a site from the map, with the help of the boys and girls in the Youth Club. Your first job is to find each of the sites, using the directions from Mr Williams (Figure 10.4).

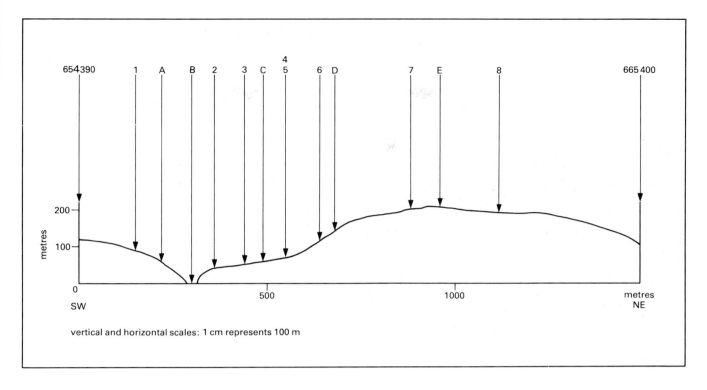

▲ Figure 10.2   Across section of the valley of the Afon Prysor

▼ Figure 10.3   Letter from Mr Williams to Stuart Lindeman

▼ Figure 10.4   Directions for finding camp sites

Felinrhyd Fach
Moel y Gryafolen
Tyn Twll
Gwynedd

Stuart Lindeman
The Beacon Youth Club
Lansdowne Road   15th February
Birmingham

Dear Stuart Lindeman,

Thank you for your letter requesting permission to
camp on my land. I can well understand your wish to
come to this beautiful part of Wales and you are
most welcome.

It would be best if you could visit the farm to
choose a site before August. I was unsure what kind
of site you might want, so I have chosen four
possible places and I have included directions for
finding each of them, on a separate sheet. As my
wife and I may be busy with work on the farm,
especially during the lambing season, perhaps you
would like to follow these directions and inspect
the sites by yourself?

Yours sincerely,

Alun Williams

(Mr Alun Williams)

Directions for finding camp sites

No doubt, you will be coming via the A496, which runs
south west beside the Afon Dwyryd. Turn left, just
before the Maentwrog Power Station. You will see a
signpost there to my farm, Felinrhyd Fach. Park at
the farm buildings where I live and walk 250 metres
uphill along the road to a gate which is across the
road.

1. Through the gate the road is unfenced and on your
right is a small, grassy field, a little under half a
hectare in size. It has an electricity pylon in the
middle. The road, as you have seen, is a public road,
despite the gates, so this may not suit you. The site
is, however, the nearest one to the mains water supply
from the farm.

2. Follow the road up the hill, crossing two streams,
to the next gate. Through this gate and on your left
is a field which is very nearly one hectare in size.
A large pipe forms its northern boundary. You could
use part of this field.

3. About 500 metres further on up the road, after
crossing the pipeline, you will find a track to your
left. It is opposite a small pond which is on the
south side of the road. The track becomes a path
after 50 metres or so and will bring you back past
Tyn-y-Coed. The path runs parallel to the pipeline
and then under two lots of electricity transmission
lines. Keep away from the disused levels. These old
mines can be dangerous! Take the path to the top of
the hill. You'll find a small patch of rough grassland
with bracken and a pond. This is a third possible camp
site.

4. The last spot is back down the same path, but this
time fork right across the stream and under the pipeline.
This field is much larger, but it is rather damp. You
might, however, find a spot somewhere in it.

To get back to your car, follow the path back to the
road and you should be able to find your way from there.

(b) Having found the four sites, decide what conditions might be important for a Youth Club summer camp. Consider such things as water supply, flat land, good views and so on, and write down your list of conditions.

(c) Choose one of these sites and write down the reasons why you chose it. Perhaps the class could become the members of the Youth Club and decide, by means of a class discussion, which is the most favoured site. Alternatively, a decision could be made by taking a class vote.

(d) You may have found that none of these sites is perfect. If so, see if you can find a better site on Mr Williams' farm. Write a short letter, trying to persuade Mr Williams to let your Youth Club use the new site that you have chosen.

(e) When the Beacon Youth Club wanted to do an exhibition about what happened on their holiday, they found three unlabelled photographs of places on the farm. Figure 10.5 was taken from 664 395 and it shows the two disused mines, or levels. Figure 10.6 was taken from the path just north of Tyn-y-Coed, looking westward. Figure 10.7 is a view of ruined buildings at Pen-y-foel, as seen from fifty metres to the east of them. Use Map 12 to locate each photograph. Then choose one of these photographs and write a short, imaginative paragraph about an incident that happened there on the holiday.

▲ Figure 10.6   The pipeline near Tyn-y-Coed

▲ Figure 10.7   Pen-y-foel

▲ Figure 10.5   Disused mines

Farmer and farm

Mr Williams is a farmer's son from Gwent and he came to Felinrhyd Fach in 1954. His wife comes from the local area and she is a farmer's daughter. Since 1954, Mr Williams has changed the farm a great deal. In particular he has bought two small neighbouring farms to make his farm larger. These old farm buildings remain at Tyn-y-Coed (668 393) and Llech-y-Cwm (671 390). However, the Williams' chose to live at the Felinrhyd Fach farm buildings. Map 12 shows how Mr Williams divides his farm into seven main sections to make the job of sheep farming easier. When his flock is in one of the sections B

Map 11

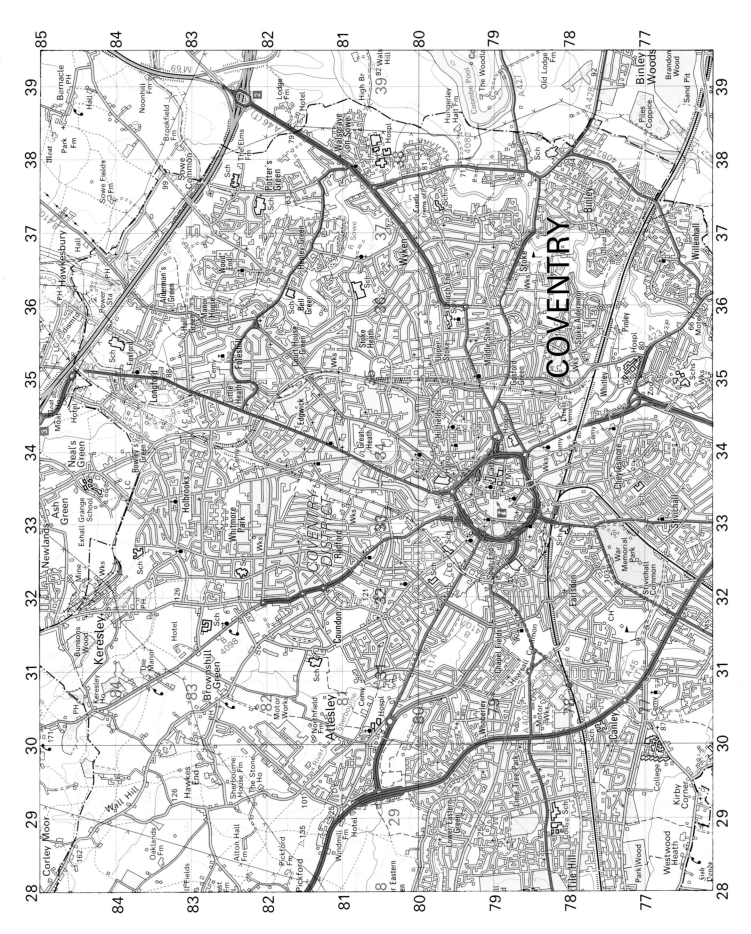

Map 12

Map 12 North Wales (1:10 000)

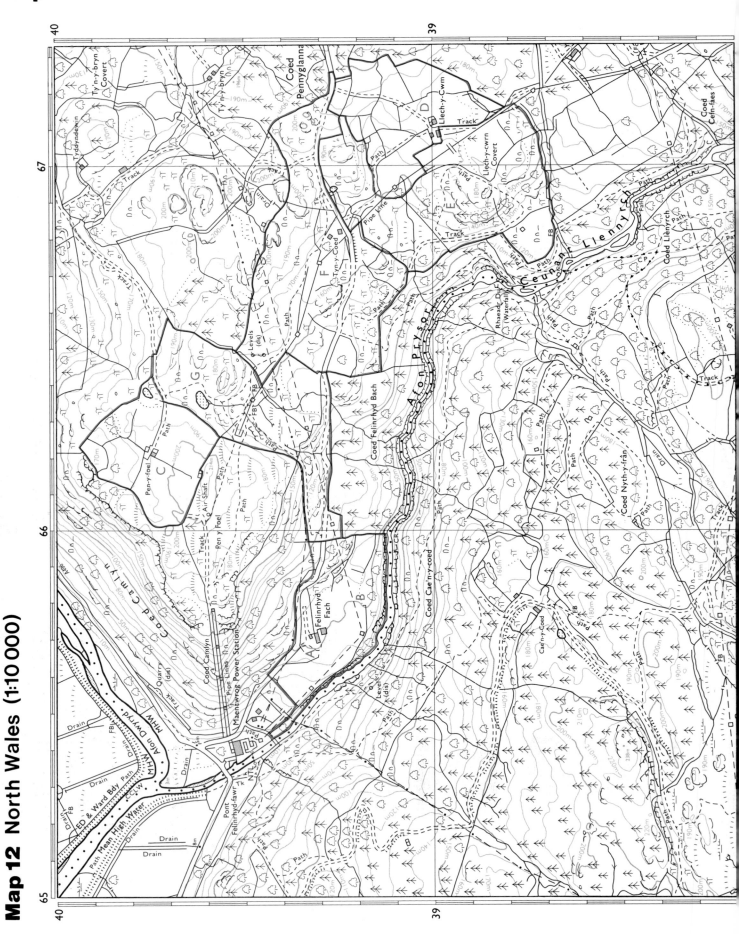

to G, he either leaves all the gates open or he drives the flock from one field to another, in that section. Map 12 can be used to get an impression of the quality of the land. For example, consider the descriptions of sections A, B, C and G in the following paragraphs.

Land quality

Section A   Felinrhyd Fach farm buildings consist of a farmhouse, two larger, general purpose barns and various smaller outbuildings.

Section B   This is probably good quality pasture. There is one main field, situated in the bottom of the valley and sloping gently towards the Afon Prysor. The farm buildings are placed in the middle of this section. There is some woodland and bracken growing on steep slopes at the edge of the field.

Section C   This is probably good pasture. This is shown by the absence of bracken, scrub, trees and rock outcrops. There are four main fields of gently sloping land on top of a hill at about 190 metres above sea level. This position means that the fields are exposed in bad weather. There are small patches of woodland and a large pond in the corner of one field.

Section G   This is mostly very poor quality pasture. The fields contain bracken, scrub and rough grassland. There is a small lake and there are several streams running through this section, one of which flows through a marsh. There are some rocky outcrops and the field by the road is particularly steep.

Activity 10:6

(a) Compare the descriptions above with the map, Map 12. Now try to write your own, brief descriptions of section D, E and F.

(b) If each section of the farm can support a flock of sheep for the same period of time, why are sections B, C and D smaller than E, F and G?

(c) 'Footrot' is a disease that causes great discomfort to sheep and it happens when sheep are kept on damp ground or on the same ground for a long period of time. Which section of the farm is the dampest? How might rocky outcrops in a field reduce the footrot problem?

Time for decisions

Mr Williams keeps Welsh Mountain sheep like those in Figures 10.8 to 10.15. They are small, active and hardy, which makes them an ideal breed for a hill farm. They make excellent meat, which is the chief reason for keeping them, though the fleece is a useful by-product. Mr Williams' year can be broken up into monthly parts. Each month means a particular job or set of jobs which he does at the same time every year. He considers his year starts in September with 'Making up the flock'.

The sheep farmer's year

September: making up the flock   This is when Mr Williams prepares his flock of 250 ewes. Each sheep is examined to see how suitable it is for breeding. Generally, about fifty old ewes, which have problems such as missing teeth and damaged udders, are chosen from the flock and sent to market. They are replaced by fifty ewe lambs that were selected from the lamb flock that was born the previous spring. This maintains a balanced flock of young and mature ewes (see Figure 10.8). Mr Williams says, 'fitness is more important than fatness, and the ewe flock ought not to be too well-fed.' The lamb flock, which is kept separately in the period September to November, continues to fatten and, as each lamb reaches market weight, it is sold.

▲ Figure 10.8   Part of a flock of breeding Welsh mountain ewes

October/November: breeding season   Five rams (see Figure 10.9) are hired for mating and they join the ewe flock for these months. Experience shows that better grazing conditions at this time will lead to more lambs being born the following spring. Generally, each ewe gives birth to one lamb each year. In October, fifty ewe lambs are chosen as suitable replacements for the fifty old ewes that will be sent to market in the following September. Mr Williams says, 'They are too young for breeding this year, so I send them off to a friend of mine in Shropshire to grow up strong and healthy on his richer pastures before rejoining the main flock in May.'

December/January/February: overwintering   It is good for in-lamb (i.e. pregnant) ewes not to gain or lose weight at first. However, nearer lambing time (i.e. when the ewes give birth) the ewes need extra feeding. Several possibilities exist. The flock can be kept on poorer pastures, later being fed hay and concentrated food (see Figure 10.10), though dangers from harsh weather and damp ground can cause sheep

▲ Figure 10.9   Three rams

▼ Figure 10.10   Overwintering on the hills

deaths and footrot. Keeping the flock on better grazing land can be done, though there is little grass growth during these months and the better ground is more easily damaged. The flock can be kept in the Felinrhyd Fach farm buildings, being fed hay and concentrated food (see Figure 10.11), though this is expensive. Lastly, a combination of these ways of managing the flock can be adopted. Mr Williams comments, 'Winters can be bad. Usually in January and February it snows heavily and life gets difficult.

March/April: lambing   Mr Williams tells us, 'This is the busiest time of my year. Day and night, in rain, snow and wind someone has to keep an eye on the sheep.' The ewes need a good diet, some concentrated food as well as grass which, fortunately, is beginning to grow in March. This is a hazardous time for newly born lambs though, and the whole flock needs a lot of attention. A good year and careful attention can ensure 95 lambs for every 100 ewes (see Figure 10.12). By feeding the flock on concentrated food as well as grass, the same farm sections can be used for two consecutive months. Damp or exposed ground though, is particularly bad for lambing.

May/June: fattening   For good, early growth, it is an advantage to keep the ewe and lamb flock on good grazing land for as long as possible. June is also the main hay-making month.

▲ Figure 10.11   Overwintering in farm buildings

▼ Figure 10.12   Lambing time

July: shearing and dipping   The grass in fields newly cut for hay is particularly nutritious and grass is growing well everywhere on the farm. In this month, fattening of the lambs continues while the ewes are sheared (see Figure 10.13) and the wool is sold locally. Alun Williams says, 'Although I can shear them myself, it is better to get a contractor in to do it. They do it quicker and more efficiently than me. We've got facilities for shearing and dipping at both Felinrhyd Fach and Llech-y-Cwm.' Dipping is done at the end of the month to prevent parasites on the sheep's wool and skin (see Figure 10.14).

August: weaning   The lambs are separated from their mothers and kept out of their hearing during this month. The lambs still need to be fed on good pasture as much as possible in August, September, October and November to gain weight before each sale. They are sold in a local market throughout September, October and November (see Figure 10.15) for about £30 each. The price drops in October and November. Things are different for the ewe flock, as Mr Williams explains: 'I want the lambs to gain weight but not the ewe flock. Fat sheep aren't good for breeding. I like mine to be fit and tough!'

Could you be a successful sheep farmer? The following activity gives you a chance to find out. You will be making some of the decisions Mr Williams has to make every year.

Activity 10:7

(a) Your task is to complete the planning chart, Figure 10.16, for the twelve months, December to November. This means making decisions about where each of the sheep farmer's jobs should take place on the farm in each month. The following points should help you. Read them all before starting.

(i) Consider the nature of the different farm sections, A to G, available to you. See the paragraphs headed 'Farmer and farm', Activity 10:6 and Map 12.
(ii) Read carefully the information about the sheep farmer's year on pages 119–22.

▲ Figure 10.13   Shearing

▲ Figure 10.14   Dipping

▲ Figure 10.15   The market

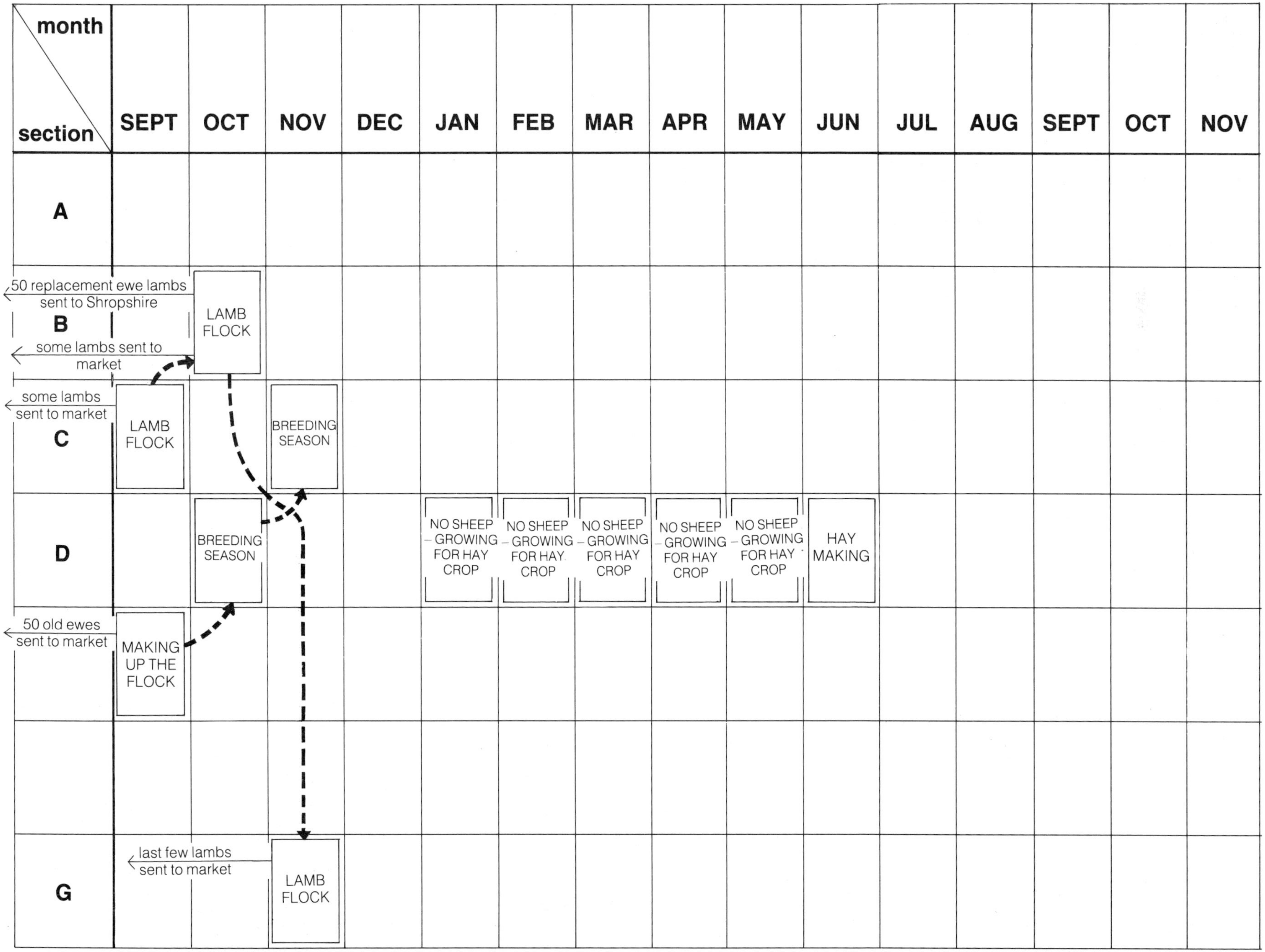

Figure 10.16 Sheep Farming Year, Planning Chart

(iii) Study Figure 10.16, The Sheep Farming Year Planning Chart. Try to decide why Mr Williams does his *making up the flock* in Section E in September. Think why he keeps the lamb flock in Section C in the same month. Now think why he moves the lamb flock to Sections B and G as the last lambs are sold in October and why the ewe flock grazes Sections D and C in the *breeding season*.

(iv) You must try to avoid keeping a flock on the same ground in months that follow on from each other. This is to avoid overgrazing and the encouragement of pests and diseases in the fields.

Keep referring to this advice as you now make the decisions where to put your flock throughout the year.

(b) The second part of this activity is to work out how successful your Sheep Farming Year Planning Chart has been. Success is shown by the number of lambs you have managed to get to market by the end of the year and the market price you receive. Your teacher will explain how to find this information.

(c) You can extend this activity by considering the following situation. If Mr Williams decided to keep the fifty replacement ewe lambs instead of sending them to Shropshire in October, his problem would be where he would graze them. Add a separate flock of *replacement ewe lambs* to the Planning Chart completed in (a). Remember that this flock needs to gain weight and strength as much as possible from October, when they were selected, until the time they rejoin the main ewe flock in May.

(d) To what extent would decisions, made in your year in charge, have affected the farming landscape?

(e) How might the effect that the farmer has on the landscape vary with the type of farming that he does? For example, how does the effect of a cereal farmer or market gardener compare with that of a sheep farmer?

Activity 10:8

Mr Williams continually tries to improve and change his farm. The decisions he makes about improvements also affect the farming landscape.

(a) Choose a field that looks particularly suitable for improvement from poor pasture. Improvement means destroying bracken, cutting scrub, felling trees and generally making the field suitable for ploughing and re-seeding with grass and clover. Explain the reasons for your choice.

(b) Which field do you think Mr Williams might consider for sale to a forestry company? Give reasons for your choice.

(c) Farming the hills of Britain is difficult and not always very profitable. Try to think of five different ways in which Mr Williams might increase his income. Be imaginative, but try to keep your ideas applicable to Felinrhyd Fach Farm.

In Activity 10:1 (e) you probably included, quite rightly, the farmers themselves as a group who influence the appearance of farming landscapes. However, did you include the politicians in the Common Market? Hill farmers like Mr Williams receive money from the Common Market to help them build new sheds and fences and also for each sheep they keep. Perhaps all the millions of pounds that go to hill farmers would be better spent on farmers in more favoured regions? 'Not so,' says Mr Williams. 'Then you would have a much smaller sheep industry in the UK and you would have vast import bills for lamb coming from abroad. More than that, the local shop, the local garage and so on, make money when we farmers buy the things we need. Without us, the local community would die. Lastly, just think how the landscape would change without us hill farmers!'

Activity 10:9

(a) Has Mr Williams got a valid point of view? Describe possible changes in the landscape that might take place if Mr Williams was forced to stop farming Felinrhyd Fach farm.

(b) On the other hand, suggest possible changes to the farm and its landscape that might take place if the EEC sheep subsidy was doubled.

(c) Argue the case that EEC money would be better used for purposes other than supporting hill farmers.

Glossary

Absolute distance A distance that has an exact, measured length.

Absolute location The words used to describe a position on the earth's surface which has been pinpointed with the use of a reference system, e.g. the grid reference system.

Area brace An 'S' shape symbol used on O.S. 1:2500 maps to link two patches of land into one land parcel for the purposes of area measurement.

Area number The figure shown on O.S. 1:1250 and 1:2500 maps indicating the area of the land parcel in which it lies.

Aspect The direction a slope faces.

Bearing The direction from one place to another measured in degrees from north.

Bench mark A point where the height above sea level has been accurately surveyed.

Compass rose A diagram which names the main directions on the earth's surface.

Contour A line on a map that joins places that are the same height above sea level.

Contour interval The difference in height between two neighbouring contours.

Crooked distance The total length of a continuous line between two points on a map which cannot be measured as a straight line.

Cross section A diagram that shows a sideways view of the relief of the earth's surface along a particular line.

Dead ground Land hidden from view in an oblique aerial photograph.

Eastings Lines in the Ordnance Survey grid reference system that run north/south on a map.

Flow diagram A drawing giving information about the movement of something from one place to another.

Grid reference system A means of locating places on maps.

Hypothermia A dangerous state of the body when its temperature becomes drastically lowered.

Key The system used to explain the symbols used on a map.

Landmarks Distinctive natural or man-made features in the landscape.

Land parcel number The number given to each parcel of land, the area of which has been measured and shown on an O.S. 1:1250 or 1:2500 map.

Landranger Map Ordnance Survey map drawn to the scale of 1:50 000.

Landscape The overall picture that you get when you look at any area of land. The area might be of any size and it includes all the natural and man-made features that you see.

Land-use map A map which shows how each piece of land is used in an area.

Location The position of something on the earth's surface.

Map A view of the world, or part of its surface, from above.

Master Survey Drawing (MSD) Ordnance Survey Surveyor's working document used to record changes which will be incorporated into revised maps.

Mental map A picture of part, or all, of the world's surface that is carried in the mind.

Nature's signposts Natural signs in our surroundings which show directions.

Northings Lines in the Ordnance Survey grid reference system that run east/west on a map.

Oblique aerial photograph A photograph taken sideways and downwards from a plane.

Ordnance Survey A British Government Organisation that makes many different sorts of maps of Britain.

Orienting a map Turning a map so that it matches the view in front of you.

Pathfinder Map An Ordnance Survey map drawn to the scale of 1:25 000.

Plan A view of a small part of the world from above. It shows a smaller area than a map.

Relative distance The comparison of distances, between any number of items using the words 'longer' or 'shorter', rather than exact measurements.

Relative height The comparison of heights of any number of items, using the words 'taller' or 'shorter', rather than exact measurements.

Relative location   The position of something on the earth's surface relating it to other places.

Routemaster Map   An Ordnance Survey map drawn to a scale of 1:250 000.

Scale   A way of enlarging or reducing things by drawing them in sizes proportional to their real size.

Sense of direction   Being able to spot clues in your surroundings and using them as a guide to finding your way.

Setting a Map   *see* orienting a map

Six-figure map reference   Six numbers which together pinpoint a place on a map.

Spot heights   Heights of points on a map which have been accurately measured.

Straight line distance   The distance on a map measured 'as the crow flies', or in a straight line.

Symbol   Symbols on maps are numbers, words, colours or drawings which stand for parts of the real world.

Vertical aerial photograph   A photograph taken from a plane looking directly downwards.

Appendix A:
Teachers Notes for Chapter 4

These notes may be copied and cut up into separate stages. Each team receives a copy of the instructions for each stage when they have completed the previous stage. The Rally Controller can halt the rally at the end of any stage or extend it by creating new stages. The Rally Controller should have a completed copy of the course and, to assess Route Penalty Points, the Controller should compare each team's tracing with this copy. The time limit for each stage can be decided by the Controller to suit the ability of the pupils.

Instructions for tracing each stage
Mark the *Start* and *Destination* on your tracing. Then number each feature in the correct place on your tracing. Choose the best route to take you from the Start to the Destination, including all these features.

STAGE ONE
Start: The bus station in Totnes (805603)
Destination: The crossroads in Berry Pomeroy (829612)
Your Route: Features to include, in this order:
1 a bridge over a river;
2 a hill to be climbed passing a hospital;
3 a road which passes a spot height (79 m) on your *left*;
4 a gentle slope down to a road junction with a spot height at 55 m;
5 a church with a tower on your *left*.

Observation Problems:
1 Give a six-figure grid reference to the point where you pass under an electricity transmission line. (1 point)
2 What is the height above sea level of your destination? (3 points)
3 What is the length of Stage One? (5 points)

STAGE TWO
Start: The crossroads in Berry Pomeroy (829612)
Destination: Grattons (809624)
Your Route: Features to include, in this order:
1 electricity transmission lines that you must pass under three times, but never on the same section of road. You may not travel on the same road twice to pass under the lines;
2 a straight section of road, 380 metres long which stays at a constant height of 53 metres;
3 a railway bridge that you must pass under;
4 a church with a tower that you must pass on your *left*.

Observation Problems:
1 Give the height of one spot height that you pass over. (1 point)
2 Give a grid reference to a point reached when you have just driven down a spur. (3 points)
3 What is the bearing, in degrees, from the crossroads where you first meet the A381 to your destination? (5 points)

STAGE THREE
Start: Grattons (809624)
Destination: The road junction immediately south of the Drill Hall (803606).
Your Route: Features to include, in this order:
1 a cross named after a metallic tree;
2 a road that passes the entrance to Buckyette;
3 a 200 metre length of road right next to a railway;
4 a place where you can buy postage stamps, on your right;
5 a hotel on your *right*;
6 one church with a tower that you will pass on your *left*;
7 a fire station on your *right*.

Observation Problems:
1 Name a bridge on your route. (1 point)
2 What is the approximate difference between the heights of the Mile Stone and Boundary Stone that you have passed on Stage Three? (3 points)
3 How many times do you cross a Parish Boundary? (5 points)

STAGE FOUR
Start: The road junction south of the Drill Hall (803606)
Destination: Dartington Hall (797627)
Your Route: Features to include, in this order:
1 three different bridges over the railway;

2 a section of road approximately 600 metres in length along which you can drive in a direction that is roughly 120° from north.

3 the shortest road route, from the end of feature 2, to a point which you know is 15 metres above sea level;

4 two sections of road around a conical hill;

5 a village named after a group of days;

6 a point that is within 200 metres of two milestones.

Observation Problems:

1 Give a bearing, in degrees, from your destination to your start. (1 point)

2 Find Figure 2.1 in your book. Mark on your route tracing the length of road you travel on that shows, clearly, on the photograph. (3 points)

3 Find out the distance from the last telephone you pass, to your destination. If you were to draw the same distance to the scale of 1:50 000, what length of line would you draw? (5 points)

Appendix B:

Teacher's Notes for Chapter 7

Table B.1 Route evaluation chart: distance and time

		Motorway	Dual Carriageway	A and B roads	Urban A & B roads	TOTAL
Your best route:						
Distance	(km)					
Time	(min)					
Route X:						
Distance	(km)	35 (22 miles)	37 (23 miles)	18 (11 miles)	—	90 (56 miles)
Time	(min)	29	40	27	—	1 hr 36 min
Route Y:						
Distance	(km)	—	26 (16 miles)	26 (16 miles)	16 (10 miles)	68 (42 miles)
Time	(min)	—	28	39	40	1 hr 47 min
Route Z:						
Distance	(km)	21 (13 miles)	—	42 (26 miles)	10 (6 miles)	73 (45 miles)
Time	(min)	18	—	63	25	1 hr 46 min

Table B.2 Route evaluation chart cost

	Standing Cost + Running Cost Total cost
Your best Route	+ =
Route X	£19.20 + (90 × 22 = £19.80) = £39.00
Route Y	£21.40 + (68 × 22 = £14.96) = £36.36
Route Z	£21.20 + (73 × 22 = £16.06) = £37.26

Appendix C

You can find out how successful you have been in Activity 10:7 by referring to this appendix. Each 'sheep farmer' starts with 200 breeding ewes. (Not included are the 50 replacement ewe lambs which are not yet old enough for breeding.) You also start with a selling price of £30 per lamb. Your decisions affect:

(i)   the number of breeding ewes;
(ii) the number of lambs born;
(iii) the selling price per lamb (i.e. a slow weight gain means a later trip to market which results in a lower price);
(iv) therefore, the total income from selling lambs.

You must compare your own completed Sheep Farming Year Planning Chart (Figure 10.16) with Table C.2. You can record the effect of your decisions on a copy of the Record of Progress, Table C.1. So, for example, Mr. Williams chose Section E for *making up the flock* in the first September. The effect of this choice for this job can be read on Table C.2. It is a good decision, so the whole ewe flock could become pregnant and selling price is unchanged. In October he placed the ewe flock in Section D, a good choice for the *breeding season*. Ninety-five ewes become pregnant. Another sound choice in November left another ninety-five ewes pregnant. (N.B. It is *not* your task to sell lambs in the *first* September to November period.)

Table C.1   Record of progress

Months	Selling price (£) in second Nov.	Number of breeding ewes (i.e. those able to/which become pregnant)	Number of lambs
September	30	200	*This year's lambs are sold by Mr Williams*
October	30	95	
November	30	190	
December			
January			
February			
March			
April			
May			
June			
July			
August			
September			
October			
November			

TOTAL INCOME = SELLING PRICE BY SECOND NOVEMBER × NUMBER OF LAMBS SOLD BY SECOND NOVEMBER

TABLE C.2 Year Planning Chart

	SEPT	OCT	NOV	DEC	JAN	FE
A	Convenient for sorting sheep, but expensive feed and grass wasted elsewhere **Effect: lose £2 per head from S.P.**	Not good surroundings for breeding **Effect: only 50 ewes become pregnant** Expensive for lamb fattening **Effect: lose £2 per lamb from S.P.**	Still a poor choice for breeding **Effect: only 50 ewes become pregnant** Poor choice for fattening last few lambs **Effect: lose £2 per lamb from S.P.**	Expensive concentrated food needed as well as hay **Effect: lose £2 per lamb from S.P.**	Expense of concentrated food needed is balanced by safer conditions and stronger lambs born in May/Apr. **Effect: no change**	Same as
B	Not a good choice for 'making up the flock'; sheep may be overfed **Effect: 20 ewes will not become pregnant. Subtract these from the total of pregnant ewes achieved by the end of November.**	↑ Fine choice for breeding **Effect: 95 ewes will become pregnant** Good fattening land for Lamb flock. **Effect: add £1 per lamb to S.P.** ↓	↑ Good choice for breeding **Effect: 95 ewes will become pregnant** Good choice for fattening last few lambs. **Effect: add £1 per lamb to S.P.** ↓	↑ Good grazing land is too easily damaged, leading to less efficient fattening later in year **Effect: lose £1 per lamb from S.P.** ↓	Good grazing land easily damaged but is less exposed and close to farm **Effect: lose £1 from S.P.**	Same as
C					Good grazing land easily damaged. Exposed situation → losses **Effect: lose 10 pregnant ewes and £1 from S.P.**	Good gra land easi aged but eases sli **Effect: lo pregnan and £1 fr
D	Good choice for Lamb Flock, weight is gained rapidly **Effect: add £1 per lamb to S.P.**				**not a choice – used for hay**	Same as
E	↑ Good choice for making up the flock; poorer pastures, steeper slopes lead to fitter flock **Effect: all 200 ewes have a chance of becoming pregnant**	↑ Poorer grazing leads to less successful breeding season **Effect: only 75 ewes become pregnant** Poor choice for Lamb flock **Effect: lose £1 per lamb from S.P.** ↓	↑ Not good for breeding **Effect: 75 ewes become pregnant** Unsuitable choice for lamb fattening **Effect: lose £1 per lamb from S.P.** ↓	↑ Best choice: plentiful rocky outcrops help sheep avoid footrot. Tougher conditions lead to fitter sheep **Effect: no change** ↓	Harsh winter means some ewes will not survive. Very poor grazing **Effect: 15 pregnant ewes die. Also lose £1 per lamb from S.P.** ↓	↑ Slightly be weather b snowfall e month stil some loss **Effect: lo pregnant and lose lamb fron
F						
G	Less rapid weight gain by lamb flock **Effect: lose £1 per lamb from S.P.** ↓			Ground is too damp, causing footrot and other problems **Effect: 10 ewes lose lambs prematurely**	Very difficult conditions **Effect: lose 15 pregnant ewes and £1 per lamb from S.P.**	↓

N.B. 1. If the same farm section (excluding A) has been used for two months which follow each other, this reduces productivity.
Effect: lose £2 from S.P.

	MAR	APR	MAY	JUNE	JUL	AUG
	...od choice for ...b survival but ...ensive feed **...ect: all ewes ...duce one ...mb each but ...e £2 from S.P.**	Same as Mar.	Expensive way to fatten sheep **Effect: lose £2 from S.P.**	Same as May	Close to shearing / dipping facilities but expensive feed **Effect: lose £2 from S.P.**	Any sheep kept indoors are expensive to feed **Effect: lose £2 from S.P.**
	...od choice ...se to farm **...ect: pregnant ...es produce ...e lamb each, ...100% of ...mbs live**	Same as Mar.	Good grazing land for fattening. **Effect: add £1 per lamb to S.P.**	Same as May	Close to shearing / dipping facilities and good grazing **Effect: add £1 to S.P.**	Good grazing for lamb flock **Effect: add £1 to S.P.**
	...tant from farm ...d very exposed ...uses lamb ...ses at birth **...ect: only 70% ...lambs live**	Same as Mar.			Far from shearing / dipping facilities, but good grazing **Effect: no change**	Poor grazing for ewe flock: they gain weight too quickly **Effect: 10 ewes will not become pregnant**
	...me as Jan.	Same as Jan.	Same as Jan.	Same as Jan.	Excellent choice: nutritious grazing and near shearing / dipping facilities **Effect: add £2 to S.P.**	
	...or for lambing, ...distant from ...m **...ect: only 80% ...nbs live**	Same as Mar.	Not good for fattening, slow weight gain by lambs **Effect: lose £1 from S.P.**	Same as May	Poor grazing but close to shearing / dipping facilities **Effect: lose £1 from S.P.**	Poor grazing for lamb flock, slow weight gain **Effect: lose £1 from S.P.** Suitable conditions for ewe flock **Effect: all ewes have a chance of becoming pregnant**
	...ry poor for ...bing, far too ...mp **...ect: only 60% ...nbs live**	Same as Mar.			Poor grazing and distant from shearing / dipping facilities **Effect: lose £2 from S.P.**	

Lambs will be distracted if kept within earshot of mothers and they will not gain weight quickly enough, therefore slower weight gain if the ewe flock and lamb flock are kept on farm sections next to each other. **Effect: lose £1 from S.P.**

2. 'S.P.' means selling price

131

Index

Acknowledgements

The author would like to thank Sue and Ed Badley, Sue Burkhill, Nick Evans and his family, A. David Hill, Brian Hodge, Geoff Morgan, Denise and Arthur Morley, Piers Newberry, Mike Powell, Mrs. E. Pritchard, Bert Sandford, Bryan Stephenson and Alun Williams. Special thanks go to all those in Dartington Hall School and Dartington Hall Trust who have helped in some way.

I owe an enormous debt of gratitude to my wife, Brenda, for all her help and support in writing this book.

Finally, the author and publishers wish to thank the following for use of illustrative material:

Collins, Publishers, for permission to quote from *The Weirdstone of Brisingamen* by Alan Garner (© Alan Garner 1960); The Post Office, for Figure 3.1; Swansea City Council for Figure 5.7; West Glamorgan County Council for Figure 5.8; Brenda Hare for Figures 4.1, 4.4, 4.5 and 4.7.

The author and publishers wish to thank the following photographic sources:

Aerofilms   pages 16, 45, 101, 102.
British Sugar Corporation   pages 86, 87.
British Petroleum   page 63 bottom right.
Cambridge University Collection   page 93.
Dartington Amenity Research Trust   pages 78, 84.
Farmers Weekly   pages 119, 120, 121, 122.
R. Hare   pages 4, 5, 10, 116
Dr G. Humphreys, Department of Geography, University of Swansea   pages 63 top and centre, 66.
Sheelah Latham   page 103 centre.
Mrs E. Pritchard   page 114.
Jim Turner   page 103 top and bottom
West Glamorgan County Council page 63 bottom left.